RETIRE WITH FREEDOM & CONFIDENCE

Other Books by Kevin Guttman

The Swiss Army Knife of Retirement Cash Flow: Stories of Freedom & Assurance to Put Your Mind at Ease

****

Relax in Retirement: Conversations with Denver Professionals on Maximizing Your Sunset Years

RETIRE
WITH FREEDOM & CONFIDENCE

Insights from Colorado Springs
experts on living the life
YOU DESERVE

KEVIN A. GUTTMAN, M.A.

Sale of this book without a front cover may be unauthorized. If this book is coverless, it may have been reported to the publisher as "unsold or destroyed" and neither the author nor the publisher have received payment for it.

No part of this publication may be reproduced, stored in a retrieval system, or transmitted in any form or by any means, electronic, mechanical, photocopying, recording, or otherwise, without the prior written permission of the Publisher. Requests to the Publisher for permission should be sent to BMD Publishing, 5888 Main Street, Williamsville, NY 14221.

BMDPublishing@MarketDominationLLC.com
MarketDominationLLC.com

BMD Publishing CEO: Seth Greene
Editorial Management: Bruce Corris
Technical Editor, Cover Art & Layout: Kristin Watt

Copyright © 2017 Kevin Guttman
BMD Publishing
All Rights Reserved

ISBN # 978-1975600648

Printed in the United States of America

The stories contained in this book are for illustration purposes only. The persons depicted herein are fictional and any resemblance to actual persons is a coincidence.

Every situation is unique. This book does not constitute financial or tax advice. Please consult a financial advisor or tax advisor regarding your specific situation. Reverse mortgage borrowers are required to obtain a counseling certificate by attending a one-hour counseling session with a HUD-approved agency. At least one borrower must be at least 62 years old. This is not an offer to enter into an agreement. Not all customers will qualify. Information, rates and programs are subject to change without notice. All products are subject to underwriting and property approval. Other restrictions and limitations may apply.

DEDICATION

To all the professionals who serve seniors and their children, thank you for your service!

ACKNOWLEDGMENTS

I am where I am today because of my family. My parents taught me to honor my elders, for which I am grateful. My wife Sabrena and children, Rachel, Garrett and Janee, Anna, Natalie and Abigail make life worth living. Thank you for all of your encouragement and support.

This book wouldn't have been possible without the help from the Market Domination LLC team. I am grateful to them for their dedication and hard work.

I want to thank every teacher, coach and counselor I have ever had. You made a difference and I am grateful.

I'm thankful for the many seniors who entered my life as reverse mortgage clients, and stayed as friends. I've learned much from you.

This book is dedicated to the hard working, freedom loving, God fearing senior American homeowners who still have dreams they want to live out and leave a legacy for their families. May this book give you hope and show you that it's possible.

The idea behind this book was to interview top professionals from different industries who serve seniors who are approaching retirement or already retired. As the interviews were conducted, I was blown away by the expertise these people shared, and the care they have for seniors.

This book is chock full of nuggets seniors and their families can use regarding taxes, real estate, Medicare, long-term care insurance, estate planning and elder care law. Because no matter what your age, too often people aren't even aware of the benefits available to them or how to access them.

The contributors to this book are at the top of their profession. I am grateful for their wisdom, insights and willingness to share their knowledge from years of experience with seniors in our community. My hope is that you will use the information in this book, and reach out to these caring advocates, so you can enjoy your golden years.

TABLE OF CONTENTS

ACKNOWLEDGMENTS vii
CHAPTER 1: Meet Kevin Guttman,
        Reverse Mortgage Planner 1
CHAPTER 2: Darian Andreson, Tax Advisor 11
CHAPTER 3: Doug Goldberg, Estate Planning Attorney 27
CHAPTER 4: Jamie Bartels-Giddings, Financial Planner 45
CHAPTER 5: Brian Canady, Realtor for Seniors 57
CHAPTER 6: Robert Edgin, Financial Planner 79
CHAPTER 7: Marcia Williams, Medicare Representative 95
CHAPTER 8: Cavin Harper, Sr. Advocate 113
CHAPTER 9: Tom Rasmussen,
        Long-Term Care Insurance Advisor 129
CHAPTER 10: Linda Leitz, Financial Planner 153
CHAPTER 11: Hayden Gregory, Enrolled Agent 175
CHAPTER 12: Tom & Kym Welton, Financial Planners 189
CHAPTER 13: Debby Miller, Enrolled Agent 211
CHAPTER 14: Bill Hall,
        Long-Term Care Insurance Advisor 227
CHAPTER 15: Ethan Rector, Estate Planning Attorney 241
CHAPTER 16: Ralph Siebert, Insurance Advisor 259
CHAPTER 17: Kelsie Heermans, Senior Advocate 277
CLOSING THOUGHTS 289

CHAPTER 1

Meet Kevin Guttman

Before you hear from all the experts who were so willing to share valuable insights and information, I'd like you to hear from me. Who is Kevin Guttman? How did I get to this point in my life and my career? Why am I the one doing this book? And how did I develop such a passion for helping senior citizens live the retirement lifestyle they deserve?

I've been around real estate most of my life. You could say it's in my blood. My parents were in real estate. They were realtors, and they invested in properties. They flipped homes long before that's what it was called. As a little boy, I used to go with my dad to look at properties he was considering buying. I learned very young all about "location, location, location." Don't buy a house on a street with a double yellow line. Buy near schools, parks and shopping. Buy in good areas where people want to live. Always buy a three bed, two bath or bigger. Most important, buy the cheapest house in the best neighborhood.

When I got older, my brother and I worked for our dad, fixing up the homes. So I learned a lot about home renovation, and how to get the most out of your investment. We were able to help him get some big increases in value with minimal investment.

Since my parents were both realtors, many nights that was the topic of conversation at the dinner table. We talked about the transactions they were working on, the clients they were helping, and all the different people they were working with.

Lenders, home inspectors, other realtors, and so on. It was a great education. Just hearing all those stories over the years gave me a real understanding of real estate. How it works, how important it is to people, and how it's such a key investment.

But I didn't go right into real estate as my career. I took a very roundabout path to get here. It was a path that took me around the world. When I first graduated from grad school, I joined a non-profit. It was an organization that helped people in very poor parts of the world. We helped them have clean water, schools for their children, medical clinics, and micro-enterprise business loans. I traveled throughout the country to raise money for these projects. And I was fortunate enough to travel around the world to see the work these people were doing. I counted it up the other day, I've been to 40 countries.

Growing up in America, we have no idea how poor some people are. Many have just one meal a day, and that one's not very filling. The lack of clean water. The lack of medical care. It was a very humbling experience. Millions and millions of people, more than a third of the developing world, live that way. So knowing how much we were helping them was incredibly satisfying work.

Of course it's also not the best-paying work. And after a certain point, I knew I had to leave that position and do something else. By then, my wife and I had our five children, and it was getting harder and harder to support my family. Plus the travel was getting difficult. I was gone half the time.

Let me tell you a little about my family. My wife Sabrena and I met in college and have been married since 1988. We have four daughters and a son, all born in the 90s. I'm very fortunate because we're all very close and connected. We look out for each other and help each other and cheer each other on. The kids are all on very different and interesting career paths. One is starting a business, one is training to be a firefighter, another is studying to be an aircraft mechanic, the fourth wants to start her own women's clothing line, and our youngest wants to be a chef. Despite my background, no one is pursuing real estate. At least not yet.

But as I said, real estate is in my blood. So when I left the non-profit world, I went into the profession I grew up in. At first, my wife and I followed in my dad's footsteps and started flipping homes. We enjoyed it, and made some money, but as many people know, it's a ton of work. And creating safe, affordable housing for people is very challenging. There's such a fine line between successfully flipping and really flopping. It is also extremely competitive.

So I transitioned into the mortgage business in 2004. And I discovered it was a great way to help people. I enjoy educating people. And if you're doing mortgages the right way, a big part of the process is helping people understand their options in the biggest financial decision they'll make in their life. I enjoyed educating my clients and helping them make good choices. After the first year, I worked strictly by referral, and was getting plenty of new business. So I was supporting my family and I was helping people. What a great combination.

Ironically, it was early in my new career that I first was exposed to reverse mortgages. Back in 2006 I went so far as to undergo training. But there were things about it that I wasn't sold on. I didn't think it was truly the best option for the client. So I put it on the back burner and waited.

But then a few years ago, those things started to change. The FHA put in some new guidelines, and I liked the changes I saw. So I went through training again in 2015, and discovered that it had changed a lot. The product improved and it was a better option for many people. I also found that I really enjoyed that age group. I like seniors. I like their values, I like what they stand for, and I like who they are.

When I went through that training there were more than 100 people in my class with our company. Fewer than 10% are still doing reverse mortgages today. The fact is, they aren't easy to do. They can be very challenging. It's a different way to think, and a longer process to get the loans through. Because of their age and situation, and because this isn't as pressing as a mortgage for when you buy a home, the clients tend to take more time. They tend to need more time to think about it and process it. They want to talk to their kids, their friends or their advisors. That can be frustrating for some of my colleagues. But I don't mind. I just work with people at the pace that's comfortable for them.

And again, education is a big part of it. There's a lot of misinformation out there surrounding reverse mortgages, so it's important to make sure people know the facts, and see just how this can make their lives and retirement better.

I think that's really why I'm drawn to it, because I truly feel I'm making a difference for people. I think about one client in particular. An elderly woman who had been referred to me by her daughter. I sat with here and got to know her a little, and I asked her, "Why do you want to do this? How can this help you?" She said, "Well, I have a duplex. I live on one side and I rent out the other. I'm 84 years old, I live by myself, and I still have a mortgage payment. It sure would be good if I didn't have that." So I asked her about her budget and her cash flow situation. Her answer stunned me. She said, "To be honest, I have to use credit cards to buy food." All she had for income was Social Security and the rental income from the other half of the duplex. So once she paid her mortgage, she didn't have much left. So we got her a reverse mortgage, which eliminated her mortgage payment and provided her the monthly cash flow she badly needed. She was able to pay off her credit cards and is now living comfortably. Imagine, she owned rental property, but she was barely treading water. Alleviating the pressure of her monthly mortgage payment was a game changer for her.

Another woman came to me and said, "My dad just died. I've moved in with my mother because she has dementia and I need to take care of her. I hope Mom can stay in her home, but I'm not sure we can afford it." When her father died, his Social Security went away. They didn't have enough money to live on. So we closed that loan and eliminated the mortgage payment, and they can stay in the home.

Stories like that reinforce why I do this. Some seniors get a reverse mortgage to buy a second home, or travel, but for many, this just makes a real difference in their lives and lets them live the lifestyle they need and age in place without worrying about how to pay for it.

Many times when a senior citizen comes into my office I say, "Ma'am, it's not easy getting old, this getting old stuff just isn't for the faint of heart." They have all kinds of health issues and challenges, and they're afraid of prices going up, and they're on a fixed income, and they have all this uncertainty surrounding them. This is a way that we can just help them sleep better at night. In fact, I've had clients tell me just that. Just recently I closed a loan for a woman and she said, "Do you know what this has done for me? I can sleep at night. I don't have to worry about money any more. I don't have to worry about this mortgage payment anymore." We always tell people, as long as you maintain the home, live in it six months or more a year, and pay the property taxes and homeowner's insurance, you won't have a monthly mortgage payment. A mortgage payment is optional. You don't have to have one. That's a big deal for a senior to have that gone.

Let me tell one last story. I helped a couple buy a home last December. They were moving back to Colorado Springs from Arkansas to be near their family. The husband was on oxygen. He didn't look bad, but he wasn't doing well. Two weeks ago, she called me up and said, "Do you remember me?" I said, "Of course." She said "Well, my husband just died two weeks ago. Now, you told us as long as we live in the house, maintain it, pay the property tax, and insurance, we won't have a mortgage payment. Is that right?" I said, "Yes, Ma'am." She said, "Well, I've got this statement," because every month a mortgage service center sends a statement. She said, "Can I bring this statement in and have you help me understand it?" I said, "Sure." She came in and we went through it and I made sure she understood how to read it. Afterward, she said, "I just need to let you know, the only way I can afford to live in my house is to not have a mortgage payment and you have no idea how much you've helped us." When I have stories like that, I just say, "Wow, I really am helping people." It's very rewarding. It's very satisfying.

I know with regular mortgages you help people, but it seems the traditional mortgage market has been reduced to rates and fees. But there's so much more to helping people get a loan than rates and fees, that reducing it to those factors alone kind of cheapens it. It's like Geico, 15 minutes will save you 15% or more. There's a lot more to insurance than that. The same with mortgages. What you see online isn't necessarily all there is to it. Doing reverse mortgages suits me well because my clients seem to actually want to sit down and have a conversation. They want to get to know you, and you want to get to know them, and I like that. I like knowing my clients and I like understanding their situation and what's going on with their family and how we can help them. I really like it a lot.

I also like the fact that it's a very challenging industry. Trying to explain a complex transaction like this to people, it's like reverse thinking. They don't naturally think this way. That's challenging.

The other thing that's difficult with it is there's a lot of misperceptions out there. Some is outdated, some is just wrong. A lot of people just get something stuck in their mind, and it's tough to overcome. For example, the number one question people ask me is, "I have to turn my house over to the lender, right?" The answer, of course, is "No, that doesn't happen. That never happens." The homeowner remains on title the whole time.

There are all these things people believe that aren't true. Many won't even take the time to learn the reality. And if they are willing to take the time, it can be an uphill climb to get them to learn and understand this product. Again, it's a challenge I enjoy taking on, because it's worth it in the end. There are so many misconceptions about reverse mortgages. I'll clear them up for you later in this book.

We often refer to a reverse mortgage as a Swiss Army Knife type of financial tool because it does so many things. It increases cash flow and eliminates a monthly mortgage payment. It can help pay medical costs or for long-term care. It can help somebody fulfill a lifelong dream. It can help them leave a legacy for their family. We see people pull money out to buy a second home or vacation home and they don't have a mortgage payment on either house. There are so many different ways the proceeds can be used.

It's been known as a loan of last resort. But now we're seeing wealthy people take advantage of it. Let me tell you about a man who was in my office a few months ago. He told me that he had paid off his house, which was worth $400,000. I congratulated him, not everyone has done that. But then I said, "Let me ask you. What's the return of investment on your equity?" He told me about how the house had appreciated in value. I said "No, I am asking about the equity.

What's your return on your investment?" He thought about for a minute, and then said "Zero". That's the point. Some people are okay with that. They don't want a mortgage payment. But this man knows how to leverage money, and this realization just ate away at him. He came back and said, "I want to put my money to work for me."

This was a man looking to get the most out of his assets. For many other seniors, the biggest issue they face during retirement is uncertainty. "How long am I going to live? What's the quality of my life going to be?" and "Do I have enough money?" They worry about inflation. They worry their medical costs will go up. They worry about the type of care they'll need as they get older. For many people, retirement is the perfect storm of financial uncertainty. They're on a limited income and they're spending down their savings. In many cases, the amount going out is a lot larger than the amount coming in. These circumstances weigh heavily on them. When we can alleviate some of the pressure, it's a life changer. It brings me such joy when they realize that problem is no longer hanging over them.

That's why I'm writing this book. To help change lives. The professionals I've interviewed, such as financial planners, attorneys, CPAs, and insurance people, work with seniors on a regular basis. They're sharing their knowledge and experience. They're sharing the ideas they've had and the tools they've used. This book is a wonderful resource guide for seniors, those who are retired and those who are approaching retirement. It's also valuable for their kids. Because as our parents get older, roles get reversed. Throughout our lives, our parents are the ones we turn to for answers. For many seniors, this is the time they go to their kids and say "What do you think of this?"

I can tell you, you'll learn so much from these interviews. I know I did. In addition to all the expertise they shared, I learned there are a lot of great people in our city who care deeply about seniors, and want to do the right thing for them. They want to make sure our seniors are not taken advantage of. Some don't even care if they get paid. They just want to make sure these people are served well. It's very comforting to know that.

There are many resources for people but they don't know about them. This book will help guide you to them. You can imagine how frustrating it is to talk to someone who can't help you, or you don't feel comfortable with that person, or sometimes you just don't trust them. The people in this book are the ones you can trust. They're experts in their field, and they want to do the right thing.

Whoever reads this book is tapping into all this brainpower. You're getting the knowledge you need to take advantage of different resources and make better decisions. So let's get started!

CHAPTER 2

Darian Andreson

Darian Andreson is the president and CEO of Senior Tax Advisory Group in Colorado Springs, which prepares taxes, provides financial advice, and brings legal solutions to seniors. It brings elder care attorneys, CPA's, a brokerage firm, and insurance practice all together under one roof. Through his self-developed seminar system, his company has developed a base of more than 950 financial clients. Darian specializes in indexed annuities, and has helped his clients purchase more than $350 million dollars worth. He's been married to his junior high sweetheart for 23 years. They have two children. Darian enjoys spending time with his family, RVing, snowboarding, and riding his custom motorcycle.

Kevin: I'm with Darian Andreson with Senior Tax Advisory Group. He's the founder and president. Thanks for taking some time to meet with me, Darian.

Darian: Thank you Kevin, I appreciate it.

Kevin: We always like to find out where you've come from, so tell us a little bit about where you grew up and what your childhood was like.

Darian: I grew up in South Dakota. I've been with my wife since eighth grade and we have two children. We moved from South Dakota to Colorado around 20 years ago. I've been in sales all my life. My wife was in the medical field. She went to college to do scanning of people's veins. She got a job at Memorial Hospital, that's why we moved here. At that time I was selling spas and I could go all across the country and get people into hot water. On a serious note, we know being on the road is not good on relationships, so I quickly changed that and found a friend of mine down at Paine Webber and he got me into financial planning. We got to New York, I got some licenses, had to make a one-year commitment and I hated it.

Kevin: You didn't like financial planning.

Darian: I was dreading it. I hated the phone, cold calling and such, but I had made a year's commitment. During that year I met an individual out in Denver. I appreciate him still to this day. I'll send him a Christmas card every year. Larry Gustafson said, "Darian, if you're going to do any kind of financial planning, stick in one area and become great at it." At the age of 24 I got into retirement planning for seniors and was laughed at a little bit, but time proves all truths, Kevin.

Kevin: Yes.

Darian: Today we have a successful company.

Kevin: Tell us how you got to this point. How did you end up starting Senior Tax Advisory Group?

Darian: I started Senior Tax Advisory Group because like many independent financial advisors, I was having a hard time struggling with marketing. I learned that if you look at investments from a tax advisory point of view, you can really help people out a lot more. And what's the one thing that has to get done every year for people? Taxes. In 2002, we formed Senior Tax Advisory Group. We did 110 taxes our first year. This year we'll do over 1,300. We have well over 900 clients on the planning side.

I really stumbled into this, because when I got started in the business, I went into debt really fast, so my wife and I had to become our own mailing house. I started doing seminars and we did all of our own licking, sticking, stamping, all that good stuff for a couple of years to get us back to square one. But you do what you've got to do, Kevin. I was committed to the business, being $60,000 in debt on my mother's credit card. Thanks, Mom. Now it's all been repaid. Now they live in my lower level, so it's been repaid 10 times over. Most important, she had a lot of belief in me to do that. We stumbled into senior tax reform, the company that said, "Hey, if you could have attorneys, financial advisors and CPAs all under the same roof, working for the same client together, the client's going to win."

Kevin: You really have a more comprehensive or holistic approach to somebody's financial picture, not just their tax picture.

Darian: Yes, absolutely, because it takes everything. When you're looking at retirement planning, it takes everything from the legal side, the financial side and of course, the tax side, which so many people are scared about.

Kevin: How are a senior's taxes different than just a normal working person?

Darian: Most people think when they retire, their taxes are going to go down, but so often they don't. When you're working, the size of your tax return depends on a couple of things. How hard you worked for your wages and any investment or business income that you have. A senior has done that work all of their life and now they're using pensions, Social Security and other retirement income. That's fixed income and so many people are not aware that Social Security is double taxed. We'll do a lot of educational workshops, getting in front of our clients or other people to tell them why seniors have a different viewpoint, why their tax return is a little different than others. It also gives you the ability to do planning, because if they're under the age of 70, we could have some opportunity for Roth conversions if they're in a low tax bracket. My parents take money out of their IRA tax-free every year because they don't have any pension income and their fixed income is lower than the threshold.

Kevin: Ah. So it was structured properly.

Darian: Yes. I was on the radio a couple of years ago and I did the math. A married couple today can make $72,000 of fixed income and still be at a zero tax return.

Kevin: Wow. There are a lot of people who need to know how to do that. With my business, I find a lot of people are skimping, or living on less because they don't want to get in the next tax bracket.

Darian: They live what I call the "what if" type of retirement. "What if something comes up? I have this money set aside for that." If people would really understand that assets don't make you happy, income does. For the last six month at my workshops I've been asking everybody this general question. "If I could give you $2 million today, or $20,000 a month for the rest of your life, which would you take?" What do you think people say?

Kevin: I think they say the $2 million, but the better answer's the $20,000.

Darian: 98% of the people say the $20,000 a month and not the $2 million. Here's why. Because these people are retired, they have the assets, but they don't have the enjoyment of having fun. If you had that $20,000 a month coming in every month, you wouldn't worry about where you're going next. You'd just go. There's a difference. If I have the $2 million, I've got to carve this out for that, and that out for this, and all of a sudden you're living a "what if" retirement. I think that's true and where we specialize in is the income planning and creating a better lifestyle. I say, "Don't live life with a little L, live it with a big L." Most people can, they just don't understand it.

Kevin: Right. So you help them get there.

Darian: I try.

Kevin: Darian, what do you wish you knew when you started that you know now?

Darian: Oh wow, they say hindsight's always 20/20. When I started, I didn't know as much about income planning as I do today. Income planning by far is the biggest need that comes across our desk. The cost of life is going up more than their retirement pay. When I got into the business, I didn't know anything about income planning and the unique ways to it. Now we understand there are so many ways to do income planning for people with the assets they have and the IRAs. It's through good tax planning, a lot of times you don't have to pay taxes or you pay a reduced tax. Money saved is money earned.

If you ask a senior who their most trusted advisor is, a CPA, an attorney, or a financial advisor, 90% of them will tell you the CPA. Because the CPA is only selling some service. The other people want to sell you an investment or they want to sell you a legal plan, the CPA just provides service and advice.

Kevin: Interesting.

Darian: That was essentially one of the biggest reasons we got into the tax side. It was because of the trust with the advisors.

Kevin: In the book *The Millionaire Next Door* that's what he says. Those people highly trust our CPA. He's the most trusted advisor.

Darian: Absolutely right.

Kevin: Tell us about some of the highlights of your position.

Darian: I've gotten to a point where I don't see as many clients on a daily basis. I manage the 20 employees we have. I never expected I'd ever do that. I could tell you managing clients is a lot more fun than dealing with the employees. At the end of the day, this business has given me a true belief for some succession planning. It's given me the opportunity to live life with that capital L. I think time proves all truths, so everybody has to go through that school of hard knocks and that learning phase to get to where we are today, but we do a lot of business. We have on average 50 clients come through here a week. 25 to 30 per advisor. We don't work on products with them all, we work on concepts. Some of them need the attorney only. Some of them just need some tax help. Some of them need the full gamut. What I've found is some of the wealthier people, some of the larger accounts, have done the worst planning.

Kevin: Because they're so busy being successful. They forget to do the other things that are important.

Darian: It's truly a blessing, this business.

Kevin: One of the things that is important to seniors is to age in place. To stay in their home as long as possible. What do you do here at your company to help seniors do that?

Darian: That's a huge, huge concern to retirees today. There are a number of ways that we help them. We can do Medicaid planning with the attorney downstairs and protect their assets from a legal point of view. Maybe they just need to have some more income so they can pay that person to come in and do the duties of taking care of them. Again, we build and distribute a lot of income for people through good income planning and the last thing is the traditional stuff, the long-term care with the alternatives to long-term care today. A lot of life insurance today has long-term care benefits wrapped inside so no matter what, the client or the beneficiaries aren't going to get a value from that policy.

Kevin: What are some of the most common mistakes you see seniors make as they approach or are in retirement?

Darian: Their legal side generally is never done. I'd say eight out of 10 people walking through this door do not have an up-to-date legal plan. That's one of the things that's just a no-brainer in my opinion. We've got the best attorney in town, one of the cheapest prices, but more important, income planning to get them to come back to that. People are used to that fixed income when they're working. Transitioning from that working income into retirement fixed structured income, that's got to be a big struggle for people. That's where we can help them. Age in place right in their house, income planning. Again I'm going to push on that.

Kevin: Absolutely. What do you do to help solve these problems?

Darian: We design pension plans, help direct pension plans we set up for the clients. We can protect their assets so what they don't want to use for themselves they can pass to their family. If they do a little planning in the beginning and we don't have to do the planning in the 12th hour, we generally accomplish what the client wants or wishes, but if we do planning in the 12th hour, it's really a challenge.

Kevin: So they need to start sooner rather than later.

Darian: That's the best advice, Kevin. Get educated. Come to one of the workshops. It's doesn't cost you anything to get smart around here.

Kevin: What do you like best about your business, Darian?

Darian: I believe we make a difference. I believe in my heart and head that we make a difference for people that we work with. I know I make a difference for my employees. That's the biggest reward we can ever get is to make a difference in people's lives. I hope a lot of people take more vacations, Kevin.

Kevin: There you go! Is there a product or a technique or service you offer that you wish more of your senior clients knew about?

Darian: Tax planning. Looking at investments from a tax advisory viewpoint. I can't believe how many people will start Social Security at 62 or 66 or whenever and they have this big fat IRA. If they got smart, Social Security is growing at about 8% a year from 62 to 66. Reduce that big fat IRA that they're going to be required to take money from in the future, and let that Social Security grow. It does two things. It helps them out as well as helps our country, I believe.

Kevin: Talking about Social Security and again, this is not a one size fits all, but generally speaking, is it better for people to delay, as long as they can, before taking Social Security?

Darian: Generally, if you have the ability of creating another income stream or doing a hybrid retirement, doing part-time work and part-time retirement, you're so much better off deferring that Social Security because there's not another investment out there that's going to pay you that 8% compound return from 62 to 66 or 66 to 70.

Kevin: Tell us about a recent client that you helped?

Darian: I'll give you a couple stories. One was my father-in-law. Back in 2013 he came to me and said, "My CPA said I should really talk to somebody who knows tax planning." So I got a chance to look at his taxes for the first time, his 2012 taxes. After sitting down and doing a question and answer session with him, we were able to amend his tax return. Are you ready for this one? Biggest refund I've ever gotten. $112,000. Because the CPA took something as a capital gain and it shouldn't have been.

Kevin: That's a game changer.

Darian: That was a game changer for me, for him.

Kevin: That's more than most people earn in a year.

Darian: That is true. Recently, it's been a tough year for us on clients. We've had quite a few clients pass this year. We're already in double digits. Recently one of our clients passed and I didn't know their kids. When their kids came in to visit with us, it was neat to hear what their parents had said. They told us, "If you can design some sort of plan like you did for Mom and Dad, with that same kind of money, we'd be able to look at retiring." That was two weeks ago, and we're going to be able to give them the option to tell their boss when they want to stop working. That's such a good feeling that we get. Again, money doesn't give you that kind of feeling. It's the fuzzies, Kev.

Kevin: Yes. I have it too in my business. It's those intangibles that you can't put a price on. Changing someone's life.

Darian: And that's what you do in your business because you work with people who need a lot of help.

Kevin: Tell us, who's an ideal client for you?

Darian: We work with anybody over the age of 50. If they're children of clients, we'll work with them at any age. The average age of the clients that we have coming through our door is about 71.

Kevin: Is that right?

Darian: 71 years young, sir. That's right. We are limited on what type of planning we can do sometimes, because they're already taking their RMD, they're already taking the Social Security. It is a lot more difficult to do the planning.

Kevin: It goes back to what you said before. If you can get them earlier, in their 50s, you have some time before they take those distributions, or retire or whatever, you can really set them up to where money won't be a concern.

Kevin: With these ideal clients, what's the first step you want them to take?

Darian: We get a lot of our clients through referrals and we get a lot of our clients through our seminars or workshops. First step we have anybody take is bring in the last couple years of tax returns. Let's start there; let's get an understanding of the tax picture, where you're going and what you want to do. Then we'll look at your investments and find out how they're going to tailor into that desire of what you want to do and where you want to go, and basically through good communication develop a plan that's going to work. Then you just plan on doing reviews, because no retirement plan is set for life. Every year we look at this and make sure we're on track, and if we're not we have to alter a little bit. I think that's the value of a good company who is there to take care of them for a long time.

Kevin: How do you market your services now to ideal clients? How do they find you? You mentioned referrals and seminars.

Darian: We've tracked it for the last seven years. We've gotten over 50% of our business from clients giving us more money. 13% comes from referrals. Seminars and tax planning make up the difference. All the clients that we get to see for tax season, we get to offer them a planning opportunity when they're picking up their taxes. All the people that come to the seminars, we get to offer them just an opportunity to kick the tires. We throw a lot of parties and fun stuff for our clients. That might be why our clients like to give us money. We take care of our clients because our clients take care of us.

Kevin: What are some of those seminars that you offer?

Darian: *Don't Worry, Retire Happy* is the tag line on one of them.

Kevin: Do you use Social Security?

Darian: We do a lot of Social Security talks in every one of our workshops. We're actually working with Affinity right now. Affinity is a very large national organization that has senior living, independent and assisted. We're doing three workshops in there this year. We did the first one on taxes and investments. My attorney did the second one, and then my

Medicare guy's going to do the third one. I can't believe how much business has come just from the Affinity workshops that we've done. I'd like to figure out a way to make that into a moldable piece that we give to other advisors, because there are Affinity locations all over the country. The hardest thing for most advisors is getting in front of people. Knock on wood, that's the one thing we don't have a problem with. I don't know if it's because we believe that our clients need to come in twice a year to visit with us, if it's the parties, if it's the taxes. I figure it's a combination of everything and giving good service. Being accountable when you mess up.

Kevin: Saving them $112,000. That helps.

Darian: That made him a client for life.

Kevin: Darian, what's the biggest challenge you're facing right now?

Darian: Staffing. Finding the staff that wants to work. So many people, they're really good at what they do but they don't show up enough to get it done. There are people that show up every day, but don't have the talent to get it done. We just want our people to show up and try. Every one of our people. I think turnover's the killer for any business. We don't have turnover here.

Kevin: That's great.

Darian: Kathy, she's been with me eleven years. She became a business partner. I brought her into the business. When you find good people you've got to keep them.

I think some of the challenges that I face coming up are marketing, from the standpoint of the Internet. I don't like computers. I'm a nose to nose and toes to toes boy. My way of doing marketing is becoming less and less, and the new technology way is becoming more and more. I fear that, but I've learned to embrace it. As you can see I've got three monitors in my office and I try really hard to get this stuff down, but at the end of the day, technology scares me because I don't like to give away the control.

Kevin: At the end of the day, we're in the people business, right?

Darian: We are.

Kevin: And we've got to stand face to face. I tell people, you know you're making in my case, a couple hundred thousand, $300,000 decision. You don't want to do that over the phone or the Internet or email. You want to meet somebody. You want to look him in the eye, right?

Darian: You would think so.

Kevin: Big decision.

Darian: You would think so. Mattress Firm just launched a new bedding line and they sold $40,000 the first day online.

Kevin: I get the convenience. But buying a mattress is a lot different than planning your retirement.

Darian: Yes sir. Yes it is. The internet's a great way to get educated, but again at the end of the day, you want to look that person in the eye and be able to see if they're being honest and ethical.

Kevin: It's funny, like in my business I have people tell me, "You know I did that research with such and such company on TV and got some questions answered, but when it came down to it, I wanted to sit down with somebody and meet them face to face, look them in the eye." I tell them, "Yes, that's the best way to do it."

Darian: That's when some companies have to bow out because that's the only marketing plan they have. Believe it or not, there are some people that do retirement planning the same way on the Internet.

Kevin: That's not how I choose to do it. What's the best advice you ever received?

Darian: You're going to laugh, simple things mean a lot to me. God gave you two ears and one mouth for a doggone good reason. Some of the best advice I've ever had.

Kevin: Listen more than you talk.

Darian: People love to talk about themselves. If you can get them talking about themselves, Kevin, you can build a relationship with them. But you've got to listen to what they're saying and not just hear what they're saying because if I can't remember the things that were important to you in our conversation right there, down the road I don't have much credibility. God gave me two ears and one mouth for a doggone good reason, and I got a notepad too.

Kevin: What would you like to share that I haven't already asked you?

Darian: You're doing something unique because you're talking to some businesses that are in the same field as you and in the same arena as you, for the client count you're looking at, and you're letting them talk about themselves. So now you're getting to do what I just talked about and when we can do that and we capitalize on it like you're doing, folks get with Kevin.

Kevin: It's been so rewarding and I've met so many great people. It's just been so fun. This book is full of nuggets. I really hope people go through it and glean these nuggets. You've thrown out three or four yourself today. Stuff people don't know. Huge.

Darian: Huge opportunity to help.

Kevin: Where can people go to learn more about you and Senior Tax Advisory Group?

Darian: They can go to our website at springstax.com. Like is on Facebook. Give us a call at 719-596-4844. Kick a tire, get educated. It costs nothing to get smart, folks.

Kevin: That's very good advice. Thank you so much, Darian.

Darian: Thanks very much, Kevin.

CHAPTER 3

Doug Goldberg

Douglas Goldberg is Founding Attorney and Principal at Forbush Goldberg PLLC. His practice focuses on trusts and estates, business representation, real estate and charitable giving.

Doug is the co-author of four books on estate planning, and lectures frequently on estate and business planning issues to attorneys, CPAs, financial advisors and other Colorado residents.

Doug was a professional athlete, playing baseball in the Montreal Expos organization before retiring in 1980. He has coached youth baseball, soccer and basketball in the Pikes Peak area for over 20 years. He sits on the Board of Directors of several non-profit organizations.

Doug and his wife Kitsen are the parents of three sons.

Kevin: This is Doug Goldberg, he's an estate planning attorney with Forbush Goldberg. Thanks for being willing to be a part of our project, Doug.

Doug: You bet. Thanks for having me, Kevin.

Kevin: So usually we start off just finding out where you're from, little history of how you got to where you at. So where did you grow up?

Doug: I was born in Denver and grew up in Broomfield. I went to Broomfield High School and did all my post high school education at the University of Denver.

Kevin: Wow. So you're a Colorado native?

Doug: I am. I'm second-generation, my kids are third. Both my parents were born in Denver.

Kevin: Tell us about your childhood.

Doug: I had a great childhood. I had a great mom, a great dad, and two brothers. We grew up in Broomfield, my mom and dad built a house there in the late '60s a block away from the country club. So we'd ride our bikes to the pool on a regular basis. We just had a lot of fun growing up. But I pretty much spent most of my childhood on a baseball field or a sports field of some sort. I played many different sports and just gravitated towards the baseball world. I also played football in high school.

Kevin: What did your parents do?

Doug: My dad was the VP of Human Resources at Stanley Structures. The company started in the late '50s as a pre-stressed, precast concrete manufacturer and erector. It was called Prestressed Concrete of Colorado then. They sold out in the late '70s to Stanley Works, the tool company, and became Stanley Structures. My mom was a homemaker. She raised us and took care of my dad and made sure everything worked well on the home front. I'm sure that was quite a challenge for her.

Kevin: I know before you'd gotten into law you had another career. Tell us about that.

Doug: I was fortunate to go to the University of Denver on a baseball scholarship, and after graduation I signed as a free agent with the Montreal Expos Baseball Club and played professional baseball for a year. So when people ask me, "How many jobs have you had in your whole life?" I say, "Two, and one was playing professional baseball so I'm not sure that counts as a job." But actually in the Minor Leagues it really is a job because you have long bus rides and not much money. But hey, it's still professional baseball. They're paying you to play a game. That was a great experience. When I got released, I went back to college and got my master's degree in finance.

Kevin: Now am I remembering correctly that you were Gary Carter's backup at one point?

Doug: Yes indeed. I played in the Montreal Expo organization and Gary Carter was the man. The starter on the big league club. In professional baseball, there are normally five or six levels of teams. There's the big league team, and they always have two catchers. Gary Carter was the number one there. Then they have the Triple-A team and they always have two catchers there. Then the Double-A team, then the High-A, the Short Season-A, and most have Rookie team. Every team has two or three catchers. So when I looked at the depth chart, I was twelfth. So yes, I played behind Gary Carter. I just normally don't say how far behind.

Kevin: You've been doing estate planning for a long time now. What do you wish you knew when you started that you now know?

Doug: All I've done for about the last 25 years is estate and business planning. Business owners are still my favorite clients, but nobody ever told me that they're difficult to get ahold of and track down for a meeting because they're entrepreneurs.

The other thing that I really wish somebody would've told me early on is that the practice of law is a business. It's an extremely personal business, but it's a business. At the end of the day, you've got rent, phone systems, payroll, equipment leases, and a host of other expenses. So you have to generate business to pay for everything, but at the same time you've got to really be sensitive to the fact that you're dealing with people, and you're dealing with their very intimate hopes and fears and dreams. That's a tough line and I wish somebody would've said, "This is a very different way to earn a living." I love it but, boy, it has sure been a good learning process for me, learning about people and how to translate those hopes, fears, dreams and goals into a revenue stream that can pay your bills and provide a lifestyle for your family.

Kevin: So estate planning's a pretty unique part of the law. For people who may not understand, why does somebody need an estate plan?

Doug: Estate planning is an intersection of several areas of law. It's an intersection of wills, trust, and probate law, with property and asset protection and family law.

In its purest form, estate planning is an act of love and stewardship. You really only do a small fraction of estate planning for yourself, perhaps during your disability or incapacity.

Most of the rest of the estate planning process is about control and protection for your loved ones. It's about the ability to control your property and protect your loved ones while you're alive and well, planning for what you want to happen if you become disabled or incapacitated and then when you die, leaving what you have, to whom you want, when and how you want; and doing all of that at the lowest possible cost, both in terms of time, money and heartache.

I've always focused on the stewardship aspect of estate planning. I believe that we are all stewards of what we have been blessed with here on planet Earth. Part of our stewardship obligation is to leave what we have been entrusted with to the next generation. We can do it well, or we can leave a mess for those we love.

So estate planning is this whole confluence of several areas of law, blended with your personal and spiritual life. If you don't get leave things the way you want, you basically are leaving things up to the government to sort out.

Kevin: For someone who doesn't have an estate plan, what happens when they pass?

Doug: The government controls the process. We look to the Colorado Probate Code at what we call the intestacy laws. Intestacy is just a fancy name for "I died without a will." Two thirds of Americans now die without a will, which I find absolutely amazing. Most people just don't do it. They don't want to think about dying. But to your question, we look to the state laws that control what to do with your kids, and your assets. Unfortunately, if you don't take control of the process, you miss out on leaving the personal and spiritual legacy that you can leave because the law doesn't deal with those personal matters.

Kevin: Is it accurate that estate planning is only for wealthy people?

Doug: No, that's totally inaccurate. That's one of the myths we try to dispel every day. "Estate planning" can be as simple as naming someone to help pay your bills or make medical decisions for you if you cannot make them for yourself. It might be as simple as saying, "I don't want to be kept alive by artificial means" or "I want to be an organ donor."

Typically, folks think of estate planning as being for older people and people with a lot of wealth. Most folks also think of estate planning in terms of death. But estate planning is more than "old, rich, dead." It's naming a guardian for your minor children, and it's planning for your disability. If you don't plan for disability with a simple power of attorney, and a simple HIPAA authorization, you can have a mess, a very long expensive mess.

Kevin: So like Terri Schiavo, from years ago?

Doug: Exactly. She's one of the people that we use as an example of what can happen if you don't take control of the process. One of my professional goals is to never have my client's name on a test case with either the IRS or the United States Supreme Court. So far, so good!

So, no, I think it's a mistake to believe that estate planning is death planning for old, rich folks. Everybody should be proactive and do and estate plan. My youngest client is 18. My oldest client was 103 when she died. So everybody 18 years or older should be doing an estate plan of some sort.

Kevin: Tell us about some of the highlights of your position, what you do?

Doug: I suppose the biggest highlight of my work is that I get to talk with families about things like how they've met, what they've done in their life. A similar couple of questions that you asked me. "Tell me about your childhood." Most people like to talk about their childhood. For many, there are great memories. For some, there are painful memories. People tell us a lot. They tell us things they would never tell their pastor primarily because those things are important for us to know so we can best help them.

So listening to the stories is my favorite part of my work. If I didn't get to talk to people about their lives and enjoy the stories I'd be doing something else. I love the fact that they trust us enough with their hopes and dreams and their fears too.

Kevin: One of the things that we know working with seniors is they want to age in place, they want to stay at home as long as they can. Are there things that you can do that you do in your practice to help senior's age in place?

Doug: Absolutely. One of the things that we do is to include a direction in their our power of attorney to keep them in their residence as long as possible. I also recommend that they create a personal direction letter to tell their loved ones exactly what they want and don't want, in the event they become unable to communicate. Those personal directions detail the things that they want, day to day, regarding their physical, emotional, and spiritual basis.

Kevin: Doug, would it be fair to say, people have a budget to tell their money where to go, we have a calendar to manage our time. Really what you're offering people is a way to kind of direct their life to say, "This is what I want to happen with my assets, this is going to this person, this is going to this charity," et cetera, et cetera, meaning, it's kind of an overarching and all-encompassing view of everything they've done to say, "This is what I want to happen at the end." Is that accurate?

Doug: Very accurate. If you don't choose, somebody else gets to choose for you. I remind folks that they have worked their entire life, they have made money, acquired assets, and done and experienced things. They have a certain pool of assets and body of knowledge. They have a values and belief system that they may or may not want to pass to the next generation along with assets. We have homes and cars and IRAs and investments and those things, so it's a matter of getting what you have to whom you want, when and how you want. But what most people have is more than their checkbook. We help them leave not just a financial legacy, but a personal and family legacy as well.

Kevin: That's awesome. What are some of the most common mistakes you see seniors make as they approach or are in retirement?

Doug: One of the mistakes I see most people make, not just seniors, is that they just don't do anything on the legal side of things. They plan their money down to the penny every month and don't put anything legal in writing to wrap it all together. They somehow think that "hope" is a legal strategy. They say things like,

"Well, I've told my wife," or, "I've told my son, this is what I want." But if they haven't told them in writing, it may or may not get done.

Sometimes people think that if they have to go to a lawyer, it's going to be way too expensive and it's going to take all this time. Many times they are pleasantly surprised. Maybe what they want to accomplish might be a pretty simple legal strategy. So I think the number one thing people do is they just don't do anything. I think that's especially true of seniors. They don't give themselves enough credit and tend to delegate too much to family members.

The other thing I see a great deal is that clients will do something. They'll have documents drafted and a plan put in place. They get things in order, they retitle everything correctly, and then they don't tell anybody. They don't tell the next generation, "This is what I've done, and this is why I've done it." It's frustrating for the next generation, and it's frustrating for us as lawyers, when someone dies, and he or she has directions, good documents and good strategies, but they've never told anybody. So now the family members are confused, and sometimes angry, because what is written down is not what the individual told the family members while he or she was alive. So the anger and the frustration of the non-communicative elder becomes very problematic.

Kevin: I just want to vouch for what you said. My wife and I are clients of yours, and I have found it more affordable than I thought, less time than I thought, and the money we're saving, yeah, actually, you're more than paying for yourself. So is that common?

Doug: Yes, it is quite common. Once people understand that our planning process is 100% customized for every family's unique situation, that there are many planning tools available to accomplish their planning goals, and that things take a bit of time to discuss and work through, we are able to demonstrate the real value of what we do and why we do it. In addition, we offer payment plans for families that need one so cost generally isn't a big issue.

Kevin: We were talking about the challenges of the mistakes that seniors make? How do you help them solve the problems that we've talked about?

Doug: I think the best thing we can do is ask the right questions. Going to an estate planning attorney is much like going to an eye doctor. The doctor will ask questions like, "Now, what's better for you? One or two? Three or four?" Much like we do. We ask, "Okay, here's some options to accomplish your goal. Do you like option A or option B? If you choose option A you will likely get this result. With option B you will likely get a different result." So we have a chance to discuss the tradeoffs, with different options and really fine-tune their planning.

Kevin: What do you like best about what you do?

Doug: Well, as I said, I like talking to people. I like hearing their stories, so that's my favorite part. The second thing I like is that our plans actually work when they are needed most – upon a disability or death. When a plan is designed correctly and updated on a regular basis, then when something happens, and they work well. One of the best compliments I ever got was from a client, whose spouse had died, and she was in our office with her two adult children. After about three hours, we were done settling the estate. The woman looked at me and said, "Well, what do I do now?" I said, "Go home, because we're done." And she broke down and cried and gave me a big hug. She said, "That worked exactly like my husband and I wanted it to."

She didn't know her comment was a compliment at the time but it was. We designed that plan together and they had kept it updated over the years. So watching the plan in action and seeing it work, and helping her adult child whom I had never met until that day be with his mother through that time. It's very rewarding.

Kevin: If what you can do is so transformative for a family and you mentioned about two thirds of people don't even have a will, why do you think people are so resistant to want to meet with you or talk about these kind of things?

Doug: Two reasons really. The first is that most people have never worked with a lawyer before. Unless they have been divorced, had a DUI, or gotten sued for something, most people have never been around the legal system. For those that have, most have had negative experiences. Divorce is negative, DUI is negative, and being involved in a lawsuit, on either side, is a negative experience. So when most people are thinking that they have to see an attorney to complete their estate planning, they don't know what that means, because they have no experience. If they don't know what it means our normal human nature, I think, is to fill that void with something negative. They'll think about something they saw on TV. 95% of the lawyers that they see on TV are litigators or criminal defense attorneys. So there is a misperception of what lawyers, especially estate planning lawyers, actually do.

Kevin: So they have a distorted view?

Doug: Correct. They have a distorted view of lawyers and the legal system, and what things cost and how long they take because they've never had to hire a lawyer to do anything. Estate planning, interestingly, is discretionary. If you get a DUI, or in a car accident, or get divorced, you really don't have much an option. You better darn well get a lawyer to help you walk through the situation. With estate planning, you don't have to hire a lawyer. You can do your own will. I don't think that's a good idea of course but you certainly can. So I think most folks don't have experience with lawyers. They think whatever they do is going to cost an arm and a leg, and they think things are going to take way too long.

But I think the number one reason people don't call us is because they just don't want to think or talk about dying. They say, "I'll get to that," and they just never quite do. They keep brushing it under the proverbial rug and estate planning just never gets to the top of the to-do pile.

Kevin: Is there a product, a technique or a service you offer you wish more of your clients knew about?

Doug: I wish they understood the planning process better. If people understood that estate planning is not just for the "old, rich, dead," and if they understood that they can take care of their kids and manage assets and they could do it long-term and they could do it very affordably, I think more people would get the task accomplished. So no, it's not that we have a magic product or service or technique, because that's different for every family, but I just wish that they understood the process better.

Kevin: So tell us about a recent client you helped, a senior, 60 years old or more. We don't want to know their name or anything like that, but what was the situation, what did they hope to accomplish, and how did you help?

Doug: Well that age group is the vast majority of my clients. I have 60-year-old plus clients with a net worth, including their home, of maybe three to four to five hundred thousand. We have clients in that age range with a net worth of 50-60 million. I'm going to tackle the lower end of the net worth spectrum.

I'm thinking of a particular client family we have worked with for over seventeen years. Husband and wife and two adult children, both married with children. The husband recently died. He had a successful engineering job and retired five or so years ago. The wife was a nurse, and as she was raising their boys, worked part-time. The husband got cancer and dealt with that for the last couple years of his life. They updated their planning on a regular basis and were a wonderful couple to work with. So for the last couple of years, they were in our office a lot. We were able to rework their planning, because now we knew, I'd guess, with maybe a much greater degree of certainty than we normally do, that he was going to die first. Because of that, we were able to do some great planning for her so that when he died, things moved very easily, very quickly and very smoothly. I don't think we've spent ten hours on the entire case. That's a case of about a two million dollar estate including their beautiful home, his retirement plans, investments and things like that. We were able to do some great work with them because they were engaged, they had a need, and we were able to fill that by just really working through the specifics on it.

Kevin: Let's take that couple, family. How much would you say you saved them in taxes or probate or whatever because they had a plan in place?

Doug: Well, most of the husband's net worth was in his retirement plans from his former employer. The taxes we saved them were income taxes, not estate taxes because they were well under the federal estate tax exemptions. But I believe by the time that whole retirement plan is paid out to the wife and the kids in the way that we've designed it, they will have saved at least a quarter of a million dollars in income tax.

Kevin: Let's just say, they spent over these 18 years, it's probably not even this much, but let's just say, it cost them $25,000 meeting with you and designing all this over 18 years. You saved them $250,000. So tenfold what they paid you.

Doug: Yes that's correct.

Kevin: Ten times.

Doug: I think that's a pretty good average. Higher net worth clients, you take somebody that has a taxable estate, somebody worth $11 or $12 million dollars these days, we are going to save them 40 cents on every dollar that they pay us, which is pretty good investment. Saving income taxes and putting together income tax strategies is really where we're spending a lot of our time these days, because the estate tax exemptions are so high. But many people have large retirement plans, IRAs and they have Roth IRA conversions.

By the time you pencil it all out it, it might be in excess of $250,000 for that particular family, but they also saved dozens of hours in time to settle the estate. If they wouldn't have known us and they would have had to go through the probate after his death and do all of the things that are required when someone dies, they would have spent a ton more hours trying to accomplish what we did without any certainty on the ultimate outcome. Between her two boys and her financial advisor all working together, we got everything taken care of for her. I bet we've saved her a year and a half of headache and heartache.

Kevin: Think of the grief, that year and a half, she's revisiting her husband's death every time she goes to probate, every time she has a meeting or a conversation.

Doug: Right.

Kevin: Tell us who's an ideal client for you?

Doug: An ideal client is somebody that cares about their family. Estate planning is act of love and stewardship. You don't do your estate plan for yourself. You do it for others. If you love your family and have people and causes that are dear to you, I'd love to meet you.

Kevin: What's the first step you'd want them to take?

Doug: Step One is to complete our Welcome Packet and give me some basic information about you, your family, your goals and your finances so that we can spend our initial hour and a half visiting about the important things regarding your planning rather than on things that we can take care of before the meeting. If we can get all of that work done up front, we can make our time together very productive. If you will spend a couple of hours getting that information to me a couple of days prior to our meeting, I can get properly prepared and focus on the things that are important to you. And of course, there is no charge for initial meeting.

Kevin: How do your ideal clients find you currently?

Doug: Of course we have a website, as everybody does, but the primary way that people find us is through referral. I work almost exclusively through referral by financial advisors, existing clients and friends and family.

Kevin: Doug, what's the biggest challenge you're facing right now?

Doug: That's a great question. Maybe the biggest challenge I'm facing right now is the lack of education that clients do with their loved ones, primarily their children. Trying to explain after someone has died the value of why the deceased person left an inheritance in trust where it's going to be controlled and protected from bad spending habits, divorce, lawsuits, and creditors is difficult, especially if the deceased person hasn't done any of that during their lifetime. If mom and dad haven't done the education upfront it's really very difficult for us after death. It's not a big challenge to educate clients, they get it, they understand it, they do it, but the missing link is the education of the family members, why they did what they did.

Kevin: What would you say the best advice you've ever received is?

Doug: I think the best advice I ever received was from my dad when he told me, "Get into business for yourself. Don't work for anybody. Control your own destiny." As an entrepreneur, as I've said, I've really only had two jobs in my whole life. I've always been able to set my own calendar, set my own schedule. If I need to go to a client's house, I will. If I need to work for them at eight o'clock at night I do. If they can't see me during the week, I'll see them on the weekend. It's given me a great deal of flexibility in my schedule. So being in business for myself I think was probably the best advice.

Kevin: What would you like to share that I haven't asked you?

Doug: People should not be afraid of lawyers. Many people are intimidated when they come in our office and we discuss legal strategies and talk about taxes and probate and other legal matters. I have had some very, very smart people in my office tell me, "I feel like an idiot with what we just went over." I typically respond with, "You know what, I don't have a clue how to do what you do all day, every day either. You're an oil and gas engineer? You'd have to sit for two hours and explain to me exactly what you do, because I have no idea. So it's not a matter of being intimidated, it's just that I've made different career choices than you. Neither better nor worse, it's just different. So let's figure out how we can help each other."

Secondly, I tell folks that when they are hiring a lawyer, they should ask a lot of questions. Because at the end of the day, lawyers work for clients, not the other way around. Just because a lawyer recommends something doesn't mean you should blindly say "okay." You should ask a lot of questions, and you should go in prepared. In fact, I offer people a list of questions to ask their estate planning lawyer. If they say, "I'm going to go see another lawyer," I say, "Well, let me give you some questions to ask that lawyer." It's okay to ask questions. You're in charge.

Kevin: Where can our audience go to learn more about you?

Doug: Probably the best place is our website. Forbushgoldberg.com. My bio and picture is there, they can learn about who we are and what we do, how we work, what our process is, and the expertise that we have. We've got a number of lawyers in our practice, and we've got a great support team. That's the best place for them to go. Then of course we always offer that no charge initial consultation if they're serious about doing their work, they'll fill out the welcome packet. If at the end of that, that first meeting they decide not to do anything there's no obligation. If they decide to move forward, we map out a plan for them. Bottom line, you have to be able to trust the person that you're working with.

Kevin: Awesome. Thank you, Doug.

Doug: Thanks, Kevin.

CHAPTER 4

Jamie Bartels-Giddings

Jamie Bartels-Giddings has been a financial advisor at First Command Financial Services in Colorado Springs since 2008. She is a graduate of Cameron University with a Bachelor's Degree in Business Administration, holds Series 6, 63 and 65 securities licenses plus state life and health insurance licenses, and is a member of the Financial Planning Association.

Jamie's areas of focus include comprehensive financial planning, investment strategies, retirement income planning, education funding solutions, asset allocation and management, and insurance solutions and risk management.

She is an avid volunteer in local youth sports, and a member of the American Business Women's Association, Southern Colorado Women's Chamber of Commerce and Red Cross Young Professionals. Jamie enjoys hiking, snowboarding, traveling, playing golf and spending time with her three children.

Kevin: Jamie, how did you get started in financial planning?

Jamie: When I got out of college I thought I wanted to go work for a large company, climb the corporate ladder. I started working with AIG, AIG and American General doing lending. I found out, we were doing a lot of sub-prime lending, and then I got a call from an

	old lady who needed a loan to pay her rent and car payment. I said, "This is not for me. I need to get out of here," and then I started interviewing financial-planning firms. I wanted to be more proactive and less reactive with people's financial plans and when I left AIG, that was early 2008.

Kevin: How did you get to this point now in your career?

Jamie: Hard work and determination. Being a financial advisor starting in 2008 was not easy by any means. I had a lot of people telling me I would probably not make it. I would fail, being it was 2008, I was a single mom at the time, and this was going to be my only source of income. All these people were saying, "You're not going to make it. You're not going to make it." That made persevere even more. I had some hard years because it's a commission only job, and here I am nine years later.

Kevin: What do you wish you knew when you started that you know now?

Jamie: I wish I would have known that not every action will give you the reward you want, but you have to keep doing the basic things. You have to constantly stay in communication with your clients. I know when I first started I could have communicated more with my clients. You don't want to annoy them, but you want them to know that you're always there for them, especially in a financial industry. I wish I had communicated more with clients when I first started.

Kevin: The research shows that seniors want to stay in their house as long as they can, so I have a couple of questions about that. Do you work with a lot of senior clients?

Jamie: I'm studying for what's called an RICP, which is a Retirement Income Certified Professional, because a lot of times in this industry, financial advisors, are great at accumulation. Companies don't teach that. Firms and companies don't teach distribution and how people should live off their assets. It's this ambiguous thing we know we're going to get to, but we'll deal with that in 30 to 40 years.

Kevin: What are some of the common mistakes you see people making when they're trying to age in place and not go to a nursing home?

Jamie: If they are not taking care of themselves health wise, that's going to be the number one mistake, even something as little as hiring a nurse to come out to your home and assist you with the basics. That's going to help you to stay in your home longer. There are so many products out there that will pay you cash to be able to bring somebody in and help you to do the things that you can no longer do. If you can get some assistance, you'll be able to stay in your home a lot longer and not have to go to the nursing home.

Kevin: When we do our seminars, we try to plant the seed. We say, "We don't offer these things, but you need to go talk to your financial professional because they can help you accomplish these goals you say you want."

Jamie: I've got a statistic here that I thought you'd find interesting. Twenty-eight percent of people who live to be 65 make it until age 90. Normal life expectancy right now is 81. If you live to 65, you're probably going to make it to 90. That's a long time.

Kevin: How do you help people avoid these mistakes?

Jamie: Creating their retirement income plan, discussing all the different risks. There are so many risks that are out there. You've got longevity risk, and you have inflation risk. You've got so many different types of risks, so we don't want a client to be insurance broke. I think that's one of the common fears out there is becoming broke because they're paying too many premiums worth of insurance. There are options out there to where that doesn't have to happen. Nowadays with the cost of long-term care insurance skyrocketing, there's a lot of different products out there that can really help the client to get those long-term care insurance benefits without going broke by paying the premiums.

Kevin: Tell me about a recent client that found you. How did they find you? What did they come in for? How were you able to help them?

Jamie: All my clients are going to be by referral only. I don't do any mass advertising, mass marketing, or anything like that. It's strictly by referral only. A recent client I've had that has been a First Command client for over 30 years, so longer than I've been at the company. First Command has a strategy where when they're military, that client will move physically to the next office that they get stationed out, so if they were stationed at Fort Campbell, Kentucky, they're PCSing to Fort Carson, now they're going to be in our office. This client was being moved in, referred from the previous advisor to myself. This client, he was Air Force for 25 years. Now he is a contractor working down in San Antonio.

He is about 61 years old and his wife has already retired. She retired as an RN and then she went to work for Pike's Peak Community College to be an instructor. She was older, so what happens with your employment, as you get older? She planned on working a lot longer than what happened. Pike's Peak Community College let her go because they said they weren't happy with her anymore, and Colorado is a no-fault state, right to work state.

That's another risk that's associated is employment risk. What if you get laid off sooner than you anticipated? That's a problem. We had to do a complete adjustment with their plan and say, "Okay, now you're no longer working. You do have grandkids that you want to take care of. Do you want to go back to work, or do we need to make this plan work for you so you don't have to go back to work?" Completely restructured the plan, found that she could take care of her grandkids and not have to go back to work. She was in tears in the office when she found that out because she thought she had to go back to work and now she doesn't.

Kevin: Are you seeing more and more people that have to work longer than they had hoped?

Jamie: Absolutely. We'll finish with this client's story, so now they're able to retire. She can retire earlier. We have to think outside the box. You asked are we finding that clients are going to have to work longer. A conversation I have to have with a client tomorrow, who is about to retire from the Air Force, going into a second career, so she's not quite a senior, but still needing to make sure that her retirement plan is on track. She wants to retire at age 60.

She can retire at age 60, but she needs to invest an additional thousand dollars a month. It's not in the budget. I mean, go invest a thousand dollars a month now. "Sorry, where am I going to find that bucket of money? I didn't play the Powerball last night, you know?" We just have to move things around. You've got two variables: time and money. So she invested an additional hundred dollars. She can retire at 67. That's doable, or she can decrease standard of living.

Kevin: Are you seeing that seniors are scaling back their lifestyle?

Jamie: They're concerned about outliving their money or longevity like you said. They're downsizing their style home. Trying to find a ranch in Colorado Springs is tough, because we all want a ranch in Colorado Springs so we can stay here forever. How many seniors need a 4,000-square foot house? They're potentially relocating.

I had a client who bought a timeshare in Breckenridge. He was sold on the fact that this was going to be an awesome investment. You're going to buy this timeshare, and you're going to rent it out. You're going to make so much money and guess what happened? It cost him so much money. He had to withdraw almost $300,000 from his investment accounts to keep up with this payment, that payment, the rent, the mortgage. He wasn't bringing in anything. It was a money pit, so selling off those assets that cost a lot of money as well.

Kevin: What's working for you right now to attract new business?

Jamie: I subscribe to the Supernova Advisor philosophy. That is constant communication, at least one touch a month. I call my high net worth senior clients once a month, to check in. I'm not talking any business. I call it my

HGI, how goes it? What's going on? Has anything changed? Nothing. Great. I'll talk to you soon." I send out a quarterly newsletter that says, "Here's what's going on in the markets. Here are some things to be aware of," and then I want to have face-to-face meetings.

Kevin: Each year?

Jamie: Each year, two face-to-face meetings each year, because they may not have thought about something over the phone so I may need to pull additional information out that'll come out face to face. I think the big misconception about working with a financial advisor is we put this plan into place; it's static, and never changing. That's not the case. The financial plan is very fluid. I am also doing monthly happy hours with my clients, so once a month I change the location and I change the invite list by geographical location, northeast, southwest, because traveling in this town is difficult.

Kevin: What do you like best about your business and your career?

Jamie: I love my business and my career. For me, flexibility, I work when I have client appointments. Certain days, when I do my phone appointments, I'll do that from home. I get to help people in a way that they may not get help elsewhere. I'm a fiduciary, so I have to do what's in their best interest, legally bound to do what's in their best interest.

I learn a lot from my clients. They learn some stuff from me occasionally, and building relationships, flexibility to be with my family during the summertime. I've got young boys, so Fridays I don't work. That's my stay-at-home mom day I call it.

Kevin: What's the best advice that you've ever gotten?

Jamie: I'm going to say to be a life-long learner, keep learning. Keep educating yourself. Never stop. That's probably something else I wish I would have learned earlier in my career. The importance of designations was never instilled when I first started. If you start working on designations, you're going to lose business. Your focus is going to be on the designation and you might lose business, whereas I think it's the opposite. I wish I would have known that sooner, because I'd have a lot more letters after my name.

Kevin: What do you find your biggest challenge to be?

Jamie: Not enough hours in the day. My emotional investment into clients, a lot of times I care more about their plan than they do. It's hard to let that go. You get so invested in these clients and then we deal with the death as well. We're selling life-insurance products and that's hard. The worst day is the client passing away. Those are the hardest days of this job. When you have to sit in front of a widow and help her out, you're helping her monetarily, of course, but you're helping her emotionally as well.

Kevin: Who's an ideal client for you?

Jamie: An ideal client is going to be someone mid-40s, second career, and they realize how much they need an advisor. Normally that's when it happens, mid-40s, "I don't think I'm on track. I need to find out if I'm on track. I'm in my second career. I've got a large 401(K) to roll over and I need to know if I can retire when I want." That's going to be the ideal client. Middle-class families are perfect. They may have a couple of kids. They may be younger and they may be a little bit older. Planning for education is normally incorporated into there. Lots of unique things we can do with education planning as well. Clients can use a 529 to buy a home, and have their kid rent it out from them.

Kevin: What's the first step you like them to take when they reach out to you or find you?

Jamie: The first step is to make an appointment. The first step is normally the hardest step. They don't know what to expect, so they're scared to make that initial meeting. They have no idea what to expect. They think we as a financial industry are going to judge their scenario. We're not. We've seen it all. Even if they've got a million dollars, they may think that's not enough. If they've got a quarter of a million dollars, they think that's not enough.

Kevin: Is there a threshold you start with?

Jamie: No, there's not. With our firm, there's not a minimum to come in and see us. We start wherever they're at. We build a plan and help them to accomplish their goals. The first step is the hardest step and that's making that appointment.

First appointment is going to be all fact finding. They may or may not feel comfortable bringing in all of their statements. I don't need that to do the first appointment. The first appointment is going to be know, like, and trust. Do we get along? Do we like each other? Can you trust me? That's going to be the first appointment. What are your goals? When do you want to retire? What do you need in retirement? Are there other goals? Travel?

You don't realize how young that is, and so it's, "Okay, if you want to retire at 55 this is what you need to do." Here and now, "Plan B is the realistic plan. You're retiring closer to 67, Social Security age." It's a lot more doable for the client, so we look at the two options. They know if they want this, this is what they have to do. This is kind of a more realistic option and that's what they've got to do.

Kevin: What's the best way for people to know more about you, get ahold of you? Do you have a website?

Jamie: Website: http://firstcommand.com/advisor/jbgiddings and my email is jmgiddings@firstcommand.com.

Kevin: Tell me more about First Command.

Jamie: First Command has been around for about 60 years. Chip Payne was our founder. He was in a bomber unit, an Air Force bomber unit, and he was in charge of going to the widows, saying, "Your service member passed away. Are you going to be okay?" Back then SGLI was five grand, ten grand.

Most of the time the spouse, typically the woman, was not going to be okay, and he kept seeing this, and he said, "This is not acceptable." He said, "We need to help these spouses. This SGLI is not enough." His mission, my mission, through biblical study, is to help widows and orphans, so that spouse does not have to go work at Denny's.

Older ladies, and they're probably widows, and so he started First Command and we started only working military, so for the first 30, 40 years, we only worked with military. Then we found our service members were retiring, separating, so we need to expand to civilians. I personally know military benefits inside and out. We can really incorporate those military benefits into a financial plan.

CHAPTER 5

Brian Canady

Brian Canady is a realtor at Premier Real Estate Group, where he works with his wife Tiffany. Brian is originally from Alaska. He came to Colorado after years of playing hockey and traveling around the world, including playing for Team USA in multiple tournaments. At his real estate company, he and Tiffany have grown a team and culture that promotes fun for both employees and clients. The couple has two young children.

Kevin: How did you get started in real estate?

Brian: I was a mortgage broker from 2005 to 2008; that was my first taste of the industry. My wife got into real estate about five years ago. She was very good with people so I knew she'd be good in real estate. I joined her about a year and a half after she started, to help her with the business. She was just so busy that she needed someone she could trust and that someone was me.

Kevin: How did you get to this point in your career, where you're running your own office? You've got others working for you, right?

Brian: Yes. It probably sounds cliché, but it is because of

Tony Robbins. Tiffany and I first went to his business mastery event in 2014. Then, we followed up with his *Unleash the Power Within* seminar. He talked about how to overcome your fears: the fear of failing, the fear of rejection. We learned how to handle the fear and to continue to add value to people's lives. Tiffany and I built our company by being resourceful and adding value. If we can add more value than our competition, in the end we will earn their business.

We do a lot of client appreciation stuff, trying to add value to our client's lives. We just recently rented out the movie theater for our clients. By taking care of people and doing business the right way, we could grow our database significantly and quickly. We've hired assistants and other sales agents to help us with the demands of this business. I guess that represents learning how to overcome our fear (whatever that may be) and understanding that if we fail, it'll be easier the second time.

If we fail the second time, it'll be easier the third time. We will not give up. We strive to have a good attitude and continue to add value to our clients, as well as to our employees. Our employees are a direct reflection of us. Our tagline is: "The extra mile is seldom crowded." If we can continue to treat our clients excellently and go the extra mile, and if we can do that for our employees, as well, that's helped us. That's a big reason why we've grown our business, but I like to give a lot of credit to Tony Robbins. He helped us overcome a lot of fears that we had getting into the business. We learned to put aside the fears and just bet on ourselves.

Kevin: What do you wish you knew when you got started that you now know?

Brian: I wish I knew how hard it is, how much demand is on us. We have typically 15 to 20 deals in escrow, and that's a lot of demand and a lot of moving parts. To deliver the type of service that we want, it's hard. I didn't realize that. I wish I'd spent more time and energy on my database right from the start. I probably didn't focus on them enough until a year or two in, which is still good, but we're big on taking care of our people. I wish I would've known that earlier.

Kevin: What are some of the common mistakes you see people making when they're trying to age in place and avoid nursing homes?

Brian: Well, stairs always come to mind. We have multiple senior clients that really struggle with stairs. They have a fear of nursing and senior living homes, when in reality, they're amazing facilities. You have friends there, you can go to church there, you can go eat and visit. There are so many things to do, but they have a fear of letting go of their home. I try to take some of our clients to some the senior homes we have relationships with, here in town. We take them to those places, have lunch, and try to educate them. I think the biggest mistake I see is just being uneducated.

Kevin: They don't know their options.

Brian: They don't know their options and they're too stubborn to look at options. A lot of times, we get approached by their kids and then the kids will talk to the mom and dad and have them come in. There's a misconception on how hard their home is to sell. Our market right now is an extreme sellers' market. These seniors don't understand that they can sell their home very easily for the price that they want and get into one of these senior homes to have a better quality of life. I think it comes back to the biggest thing I see, which is just being uneducated, so we do downsizing events.

I'd love to introduce them to our connection there. I try to get a lender in to talk to them about the options and provide education on reverse mortgages, since I'm not a lender. It's not right for every person, but it is an option. It could be a good option for somebody just to be educated.

Kevin: Interesting fact: Only 51% of seniors downsize. About 30% upsize and then the rest are just more lateral, so it's interesting.

Brian: Yes. It is.

Kevin: Tell me about a recent senior client. How did they find you? What did they come in for, and how do you help them?

Brian: We just closed on one recently. Most of the homes to which we get referred are by sons and daughters of seniors. Not too many seniors find us. It's the majority that the family members that find us. One recent example that comes to mind was for a client that lived in a great little neighborhood. When we went in there, it was hard to picture selling the house. There were so many things in the home.

Kevin: So, they were hoarders?

Brian: I wouldn't say hoarders. I've seen worse from other senior clients, but they just had a lot of life in there. It was really cluttered. There was stuff in the hallways and all over the walls. He had some tile that was cracked in the bathroom. Part of our listing service includes a handyman and a cleaner. We offer all of our senior clients a Blue-Ribbon Home Warranty for free, and we pay for that because we know that their service is worth it. Their furnace and water heater are usually not going to be in good shape.

For this gentleman, I brought him to one of the senior homes and he ended up moving into it. Once he moved out of his home, we had our cleaners go in. To help the client sort through his things, I brought him three types of stickers: red, yellow, and green. I told him that I wanted him to go through the house and stick a red sticker on anything he wanted to throw away, a yellow sticker on anything he wanted to donate to his family, and a green sticker on what he wanted to keep.

Then, I'd come back and check on him and see how that process was going. We got his family members, who lived here in town, to come in and take every single thing that they wanted. We had Goodwill come and pick up a lot of stuff that he wanted to donate. We had our cleaners there; I think it was about 20 to 24 hours spent cleaning it. It just needed a deep clean. We put it on the market, and it sold for $20,000 over asking price.

Kevin: You paid for all this?

Brian: We paid for all of that. We paid for all the cleaning as part of our 3% package. There are agents in this town that would donate their commission or reduce it. They should reduce it because they probably don't serve the clients like we feel that we do.

Kevin: You were going the extra mile.

Brian: We sold it, and it was just a great experience for him.

Kevin: He's a happy camper to get $20,000 more than asking price.

Brian: Typically, we do this for our new clients, but sometimes for our old clients. For someone that's been in a home a long time and has a lot of memories in a certain home, we hire a painter at Christmas time to paint an ornament of their home. He closed right around Christmas time, so we had our painter paint the home on an ornament and that brought him to tears.

Kevin: That's a great memory.

Brian: We do that for our buyers too; it's something they can remember. We do it for all our clients that would have any sentimental attachment to their home, whether they've been in there a long time, if it was their first home, or maybe it's going to be their first home. It's just a different idea, so we hire a local painter. We started it four years ago. We gave her 30 to 40 and then it was 80, and then this year, it was over 100. It's fun to be able to give the artist a nice check. It happens to be a friend of mine.

I interviewed three painters and told them what I was looking for. Then went to my friend, who is also a painter, and she blew them out of the water so I gave her the business. She charged me $15 an ornament, and it paid for her family's Christmas the last couple years, which has been an awesome feeling for us. Gratitude is one of our secret successes. We are writing thank you cards all the time. We are big believers in gratitude.

Kevin: I am, too.

Brian: We believe in saying thank you and going the extra mile. We will write a note if someone in the family had passed. We believe in focusing on the small picture with our clients and then letting the bigger picture happen. We can be in the moment and make them feel important even though the chances of them buying another home are not likely.

When they hang their ornament on the Christmas tree and their friend comes over and says, "Oh, this is cool." They can say, "Oh yeah. My realtor, he does that for me every year." We give them their house ornament the first year, and then the next year we give them another Christmas-themed hand painted ornament.

Kevin: So, they get a different ornament every year.

Brian: I give every single person an ornament every single year. It's not just the one with the home on it. They only get that their first year, but every year after, they get a hand painted ornament.

Kevin: What a cool gift.

Brian: We are just trying to go a little bit outside the box and be different. We want to be personable, add value, and be resourceful. Those are some of our main points.

Kevin: Sounds like you guys do a good job at it. What's working right now for you attracting new business? You mentioned you had some marketing online. Is that how most people find you, or is it mainly through past client referrals, or both?

Brian: So far, of the 33 that we have closed this year, 70% have come from past clients or referrals. When we take care of someone's dad or mom, first and foremost, we ask them for a review. We go the extra mile to hopefully get a five-star review from our clients. Their reviews for us doing a good job and treating their mom how they would've treated their mom goes a long way. Word of mouth is very effective. Then, 30% of clients come from online searches. We do get people that find us online for our senior homes.

There are all the apps, all the Red Fins, all these companies that are coming out and doing it for 1% and flat fees; they're inevitable. The market and the industry are changing. I still think our relationships and how we treat people will trump the majority. Yes, I have a marketing mindset.

Kevin: You believe in it and you're doing it.

Brian: I still think that treating people the way they want to be treated is how to grow a successful business. I think Tony Robbins really bashed that into our heads. We did ten days with him at one of his events. I don't know if you're familiar with them, but they're immersive. He rewires the way you think. Our income quadrupled after we spent one year with him.

Kevin: So, he was like a coach for you?

Brian: He was a mentor. He wasn't our personal coach–you must pay a million dollars for that. But we were coached by a system. We spent ten days with him, six days in a business seminar, and then four days in a personal growth seminar. It's just so powerful being in that atmosphere and seeing all these successful people who are great and humble. I was sitting and having conversations with multi-millionaires and they won't talk about themselves. All they care about is talking about me and Tiffany and how they can help us with our business and give us ideas.

One of the big beliefs that we have is, "Give to grow." The more you give, the more you grow. I joined the HBA about a year and a half ago. I was at the Christmas party this past year, and we wanted to grow our network and meet some new individuals that a lot of realtors don't think about. We try to be a little outside the box, and so we had a Christmas party. Again, my wife is the big giver here. She's had a big influence on me. A good example is once I won the 50/50 raffle, with a $20 entry, for $1,000 cash. There were probably 300 people at this Christmas party. I'm taking pictures with the prize. I'm so excited, and my wife is in my ear saying, "Give it back. You should give it back." It goes back to HBA Cares, the give-back program of HBA, which is who puts on the 50/50. The Cares program gives money to schools and the community. I could use $1,000 on December 15th. My wife says, "Give it back, give it back, give it back." She's just in my ear, I'm looking at her like she's crazy.

Kevin: Yes, it's a thousand bucks.

Brian: I felt like saying "Get away from me right now." They can see that she's telling me this and so they're kind of looking at me awkwardly, so I just hand my money back. Everyone says, "Oh, he's going to give back the money," and so they put me on their website and their blog. A week later, I get a phone call from somebody and she said, "I saw on your blog that you gave back this $1,000. You must be a good person. I need to buy a home." I said, "Okay. Well, great. I'd love to help you. What are you looking for?"

She was looking for a small investment or townhouse. So, we found her one at $130,000. So now, $1,000 turned into three grand. It turned out, that was an investment property and she's also looking for a million-dollar property. So, by giving back the $1,000, we already pocketed the three thousand, and then if we close on a million-dollar home, it will amount to upward of $30,000. It was all because I did what we believe in our hearts, that the more you give, the more you grow.

Kevin: We were talking about the model on givers gain.

Brian: We are big believers in that. People can say, "Oh, you're so lucky." Well, yes. I was probably a little lucky to win it.

Kevin: Oh, you create your luck, don't you?

Brian: You create it. Again, in our experience, the more we give and put out there, the more that it comes back to us. Maybe not right away, maybe not directly, but in some way. If it doesn't, the feeling of gratitude is so much more rewarding anyway.

Kevin: It sounds like Tony Robbins is teaching a lot of biblical principles.

Brian: He's a very Christian individual. A lot of that is who we are at our core and what we want to do with our lives and to become.

Kevin: That is tremendous! What do you like best about your real estate business?

Brian: Tiffany and I both are very relational individuals. That's why we have a couple of transaction people around us that handle a lot of our details, the dotting of the I's, and the disclosures. Tiffany and I love being around and getting to know people, and helping families get into homes. We love helping seniors get out of a home and move into a new chapter of their lives that they can enjoy. It almost rejuvenates them.

I went and visited the gentleman whom I was talking about. We do client appreciation parties, and so I wanted to make sure he and his family were invited. I get there and he pulls up in a scooter. He had a big smile on his face and was happy as can be. The house that we sold for him was a ranch with a full basement, and it was just too much for him and his family. I believe his wife had dementia; it was to the point where he had to lock the front door to keep her safe.

When I had one of my first meetings with him, we were in the kitchen talking about what the plan was, and we looked and his wife was gone. We had to get in the vehicle and drive around the neighborhood. I found her a street over walking on the sidewalk. It's just so much better to have good people around you. That's what we've tried to do here, is surround ourselves with good people, and that's what we want for any of our clients or anyone that we love. We want them to be around good people.

For this family, their moving into the senior community was just, hands down, the best decision that could've ever happened for them. In their situation, aging at home would not have been a good option. She needed help.

He was on oxygen and could only walk so fast and had to watch her. So, just seeing the smile on his face at the party was wonderful.

Kevin: I love how you put your clients first. That's so important.

Brian: One of our favorite quotes is, "Fall in love with your client and not your product." By doing that, we change our business to add value to our clients. In turn, our income grows by doing what's right, by going the extra mile. We had a different situation where the seller wouldn't cut a tree down. Well, the tree is going to fall on the roof. It's a sellers' market; the seller won't lift a finger because they probably don't have to. The next buyer would do it. They didn't have money to cut the tree down and I know that the tree was going to fall.

It had an adobe style flat roof. It had trouble written all over it. I paid $800 to have someone go out and take the tree limbs down because they couldn't afford it. They're in a $165,000 home. They needed a home and that takes away part of our commission but in the end, it's doing what's right for the client. I know that we've gotten at least one referral from that family just by them saying, "Hey, Brian and Tiffany actually care about their clients."

Afterward, we do appreciation events. The next one we're doing is bowling. We're going to rent out the whole bowling alley and have all of our clients there. Tiffany and I can just walk around and ask, "How's the family? How's little Johnny?" It is just a personal touch. That's our best marketing; by going the extra mile with our clients and letting them know that we care about them.

Kevin: How often do you conduct the client appreciation events?

Brian: We do three big ones a year. We do a movie event, where we rent out the theater. Last year, we did Disney's Jungle Book. This year, we just did Beauty and the Beast. Then, we do a bowling event in the spring. Then, the summer just is nuts. We try to put family first so we go on vacation, back to my home state of Alaska, in July. The rest of the summer is just busy.

Right around the middle of December, we have a Christmas event. We bring Santa in and then we give everybody their gifts. We have appetizers and drinks for the moms and dads and let the kids take pictures with Santa, which we send to them later.

Those are our three big events. We also do happy hours for our top ten deals. These are people that are important in our lives that we don't get to see enough because we're so busy with work. We really want to spend time with them, but those are the people that usually give us the most referrals. We want to thank people for good referrals.

We bring them in and say thank you. A lot of them are upper demographics, so we can introduce them to other trades. Sometimes we'll have other trades that we do a lot of business with come in and introduce them to our clients. We can say, "Hey, this is the person who worked on your furnace. If you ever need your furnace cleaned, this is your guy," or electricians, or different trades like that. We keep it short; two hours would be max, usually, a 4 to 6 p.m. kind of a deal, a happy hour. It's just three times a year, not everybody can make all three of those events, so the fact that we can get in front of them and thank them is a great opportunity. For a $200 expense to thank our top clients, it is a no-brainer.

Kevin: It's money well spent.

Brian: It's money very well spent. We try to do that quarterly. We send happy birthday cards and we send home anniversary cards. We're trying to do personal touches. Again, it all comes back to being different from our competition because there's enough business out here. I can just take care of my clients and focus on what I can control.

Kevin: There's enough for everybody.

Brian: There's enough for everybody and there's no need for me to say anything bad about the competition.

Kevin: The cream always rises to the top anyway.

Brian: We try to take the high road there, always focus on our clients, and really be exceptional for them. We call our employees, Danielle and Zack, our concierges. When someone signs onto our website, they don't usually talk to Tiffany and I first. They talk to Danielle and Zack. They provide good service and answer all their questions. They make sure that they have a lender, so when the client meets with Tiffany or I, the education has already started and then we take over. We like to meet our clients in the office to go through the process of buying or selling and what to expect and when to expect it.

We tell them about the fees that they're going to have. We tell them about the steps that they're going to follow. We let them know about different options they will have. We break it down up front and then when it comes to the time, it's not so hectic.

Kevin: They're not so surprised.

Brian: There are no surprises and they understand what's going to happen. I learned that when I coached kids' hockey. I tried to tell them what to do on the ice and it was just so difficult to tell them in the moment.

In hockey, you have 60 minutes on the ice. That's all. If you don't run a play in the 60 minutes, at 61 minutes you can't. It's not completely the same with buyers, but there's still a timeline. It gets frustrating, urgent and stressful for people if they don't know. With the kids, I would tell them at the beginning of practice, "Instead of being here 15 minutes early, so you can get your gear on, be here 30 minutes early. You get ready in 15 minutes, then for 15 minutes we're going to go over practice in the locker room before we're on the ice."

We'd go through the drills and I'd show them exactly what I wanted them to do. It was so much smoother, so much quicker. With real estate, we saw right away that poor planning could ruin an experience and we want them to have a great experience.

Kevin: You want to have raving fans.

Brian: Yes. We want to create raving fans. So, we get them in the office ahead of time, tell them what to expect and explain all the fees. Right now, it's a sellers' market. If we have a senior wanting to downsize from a big, $350,000 home to a $220,000 ranch with main-level living, and they're VA, well that's a hard deal. There are so many cash buyers out there at that price point. We need to educate them on how an offer is written so it's not in the heat of the moment. We say, "Okay. Well, how do we want to handle closing costs? If you ask for them, you're not going to get them, unfortunately."

Kevin: No, not now.

Brian: No. And we say, "This is a clause that we can put in," an acceleration clause, or maybe it's an appraisal or the buyer. "You're going to pay $2,000 to cover an appraisal issue." We have all these built in to try to give our clients an upper leg in this market. If we don't tell them those things up front, when we're going through an offer with them, then they're going to be so confused on closing cost and what an appraisal is and how it works.

Kevin: They won't move quick enough?

Brian: Yes, they won't move quick enough. They will say, "Okay, well what's this clause? What does this mean?" If you do the hard things first, the easier things fall into place. Don't shy away from what's hard. Do the hard things first, whether in life or business. Then, the easy things, they just take care of themselves.

Kevin: The other option for a senior might be doubling their purchasing power with a reverse mortgage.

Brian: I'm not as familiar with that as I used to be. When I was in the industry, even though I didn't do reverse mortgages, we had people that specialized in those. I would love for you to come and educate them because we do these downsizing seminars every month.

Every single event has 20 to 40 people there, of which we get 4 to 6 listing leads. They pack it, they advertise it, they feed people, they give them a tour afterwards. Tiffany and I would go in and talk about what's going on with the market and what it takes to sell a home. One of the things that we like to educate them on is if we're going to sell their home while they remain in it, they need to keep it clean in order to get top dollar for it. They can't be there during showings, and they can't have their dogs there at showings.

Kevin: It's little things, but important things.

Brian: It's little things that all of a sudden compound. I have showings multiple times a day and that's very frustrating for our seniors. They should get in and out. I have to be able to give them a mental picture of what that looks like. I can tell them a great option would be get a reverse mortgage or, if they have money, move into one of these senior homes. I'll have their home sold in two weeks. They won't be there. It'll be clean.

Kevin: They'll get more money.

Brian: They'll get more money. The $5,000 that they spend to go live in a senior home for 30 days, I'll make it on the sale of the home, especially in this market.

Kevin: And they're not inconvenienced.

Brian: Right. They can go enjoy their life.

Kevin: People say when they list their home, they feel like they're having to walk on pins and needles in their own house, right?

Brian: Yes, because they've got to keep it clean all the time. They can't live normally. A lot of them don't like that. I've had senior clients that say, "This is my home until I sell it, and I'm not moving a piece of furniture. I want to live comfortably and if they want to buy it, then they can put stuff how they want it." To which I say, "Well, okay. Your home is going to take 100 days to sell. You'll have to probably reduce the price multiple times," which winds up happening.

Kevin: With the seniors, are they a little reluctant to do updating?

Brian: Yes. Remember I said that one had broken tile? I just had my handyman fix it. It was a tile in the middle of the bathroom that was shattered and cracked and looked terrible. They just had a rug over it, which I know that people are going to lift it. I think my handyman did it for $100. In the big scheme of things, if you focus on the small things and try to take care of them, then you get $20,000 over.

It's just educating them during those events. Tiffany and I will have to say to the seller, "We're not telling you that you can't be in your home during the process, but you're not going to get as much money."

Kevin: What's the best advice you've ever received?

Brian: To add value and be resourceful.

Kevin: Currently, what's your biggest challenge?

Brian: My biggest challenge is time, demands and surrounding Tiffany and myself with people that we can trust. We need to delegate to take care of our clients the way we would take care of them. That is a process; it just takes time. We have a lot of fairly new employees. I think in six months from now, it will be a lot better because everyone will be acclimated. But, right now, just training and time are a challenge. There is not enough time in a day. My biggest challenge is just really trying to prioritize time, to delegate, and to leverage.

Kevin: Who is an ideal client for you?

Brian: An ideal client for Tiffany and I would be a senior listing their home who would be open to moving out of it and letting us go in and do our job. It's hands off, a lot of hands off, for the client. The ideal client would be someone who lets Tiffany and I do what we do best and get him or her the most money for their home.

Kevin: You want people to trust you.

Brian: Yes, which is why we focus on referrals because, your referrals are going to be the most trusting and most loyal people.

Kevin: So, you get an ideal client, what's the first step you want them to take?

Brian: I want to meet with them and I want to educate them on the process. I want to tell them how Tiffany and I work, and go over the process with them from that day until closing. We tell them what to expect from us, what they'll expect from the process, and the steps that will eventually get their home sold.

Kevin: Is there anything I haven't asked you that you want to share?

Brian: No. Again, we want to add value and be resourceful. We had the opportunity to buy a moving truck last year from one of our clients who was moving. He was our gutter guy and he got a new job that pays better. He had this truck that he wanted to sell. Tiffany and I thought, "What better way to add value and be resourceful than to get a moving truck for our clients to use?" When they buy or sell with us, they can use the truck for free. It's a way that we can add value to their lives, and add value to their family. Going forward, we would like to increase that to storage units and try to be all things real estate for our clients.

Kevin: What is the best way to get ahold of you?

Brian: Our website is buysprings.com. Our office line is 719-999-5789. My cell phone number is 719-433-1102.

Kevin: Perfect. Thank you so much for your time, Brian.

Brian: Thank you.

CHAPTER 6

Robert Edgin

Robert Edgin, ChFC, is the owner of Edgin Insurance and Financial Services in Colorado Springs. Robert specializes in retirement income, asset protection and senior finance. He is a Chartered Financial Consultant and Fiduciary Investment Adviser Representative with more than 20 years of experience.

Using a holistic (big picture) approach to retirement planning and the belief that everyone's story and goals are different and their retirement plan should be too, Robert uses a variety of tools and strategies to help each of his clients reach their personal financial goals.

Kevin: I'm speaking to Robert Edgin, of Edgin Insurance & Financial. Where did you grow up? Where are you from?

Robert: I was born in Michigan, but I've been here for longer than I can remember. I like to tell folks I'm a local even though it's cheating just a little bit.

Kevin: I like that bumper sticker, "Not a native, but got here as soon as I could."

Robert: That's right. I was around four years old when we came here. Not really much matters before then anyway. I've been here ever since.

Kevin: What was your childhood like?

Robert: It was fantastic, actually. Living in Colorado Springs has always been great. My parents are both amazing people. They divorced when I was 10. That changed things a lot. Actually, it made it pretty unique because my father did fairly well in life. My mother married a gentleman who did very poorly in life. We spent two weeks with my dad, two weeks with my mom. For two weeks of the month, we lived a very comfortable lifestyle. The other two weeks of the month, we would find ourselves hitchhiking because our car would break down. We would find ourselves eating meals that people provided for our family. Two weeks of the month, I wore new clothes and two weeks of the month, I wore clothes that we got from Goodwill.

It was a very unique, fascinating childhood, but I felt very loved in both households. Both parents supported me and did everything they could to make it the best childhood possible, even though they were very different.

Kevin: What did your parents do?

Robert: My dad was an insurance agent for Allstate. My mom, she did miscellaneous odd jobs. She was a schoolteacher at a private school for a while. She drove a school bus for a while. She was a homemaker for a long time, too.

Kevin: How many in your family?

Robert: I have one brother. I love him. We get along fantastically. We made the transition every two weeks together. We're there for each other, but we've always been the best of friends.

Kevin: That's awesome. Obviously, your dad was an insurance agent, but how did you get involved with insurance, specifically where you're at now?

Robert: Well, I like to say I started in the insurance side of things when I was in the first grade. I came home from school with a drawing of what you want to be when you grow up. There were firemen and policemen. Mine was of me wearing a suit and carrying a briefcase that said "insurance." I knew from the first grade I wanted to be in the insurance business because I saw how well my dad did and how much he loved it. I actually worked for him in the summers in elementary school, middle school, and high school. I opened up my own insurance agency at the age of 19.

Kevin: Wow.

Robert: I eventually transitioned to more of a full-service insurance and financial services office.

Kevin: Which is where you're at today.

Robert: Which is where we're at today, I'm a Chartered Financial Consultant, a ChFC. I spend the majority of my time doing financial plans, retirement planning, and Social Security planning. However, my background is on the insurance side of things. I have a lot of knowledge and I'm able to help all of the other folks in my office on a lot of the insurance questions that they have as well.

Kevin: Tell us the type of work you do with seniors. You're a financial planner, how are you able to help those folks?

Robert: I say that I am a holistic planner. I really specialize in the act or process of retirement. A lot of investment advisors are great at building up client's portfolios, but they don't necessarily know the right process or the right way to distribute those portfolios to make it last throughout a lifetime, to protect it from the hard times. We focus on not being just an investment advisor, but we really concentrate on how all of these different parts of your life in your finances fit into your retirement plan.

Kevin: That's awesome. What are some of the things you enjoy most about your position? What are some of the highlights?

Robert: Well, every client is different, every situation is different, and all of the family dynamics are different. It's a very rewarding position because we're able to help some folks who think that they won't make it through retirement, we figure out how to get it done. We are able to help folks who know they're going to have a great retirement but aren't sure how to leave a legacy. It is a very rewarding job because every day we get to show up and help people reach their goals.

Kevin: That's awesome. One of the big things with seniors is that they want to age in place. They don't want to move until they have to. What things do you do to help them remain in their homes as long as they can?

Robert: We think that one of the key factors in retirement success is having some guaranteed income sources:

pensions, Social Security, annuities, other things that can match up with their living expenses and are guaranteed, no matter what comes. Guaranteed income to cover your living expenses helps you stay in place for, pretty much, as long as you want to. You can use some other funds to grow or to provide some protection against inflation, or to have some coverage for long-term care events that might come up. You have so many different components to retirement. It is important to be able to step back and see the whole big picture or the different pieces of the puzzle. You need to be able to put those different pieces in place so that if one side of the equation is faltering a little bit, you've got three or four other pieces that are holding it up. That helps folks stay in place.

There's a lot of different products to do it, but having the right mindset going into it, I think, is more important. The plan is always more important than the products because products will come and go. Unless something big in your life changes, the plan will pretty much stay the same.

Kevin: Awesome. You mentioned some of the things answering the last question, but what type of financial assistance do you recommend to your clients? You mentioned the guaranteed income and long-term care insurance. These are all products that you can offer yourself right here in your office?

Robert: We don't offer long-term care insurance. We have some hybrid products that can help cover some long-term care expenses.

Kevin: An IUL (Indexed Universal Life) with a rider?

Robert: An IUL with a rider, but it might be better for folks to have just a true long-term care policy. It might be better for them to have an annuity that has some long-term care benefits. There is no one product that's right for everyone. We're more concerned with matching up the proper products to make sure that the plan works. In my opinion, that is a reverse mortgage. It's long-term care. It's IUL with a rider. It's annuity with a long-term care benefit. It's cash value life insurance. It could be laddering a bond fund or building a bond ladder. It could be all of these different things. A lot of them we do, some of them we do not, but that doesn't mean that they're still not important.

Kevin: Got it. As far as the seniors that you meet with, what are some of the most common mistakes you see them making as they plan for retirement and staying in their home?

Robert: First off, I would say most of them come into retirement thinking that they are still savers and not realizing that they are now spenders. They enter retirement invested far too aggressively. They don't understand or realize the importance of protecting your money, especially in the beginning years of retirement. The sequence of return risk, I try to explain to all of our clients, is one of the biggest retirement risks you can face. Longevity is the second biggest risk because it just compounds all of the other things. The longer you live, the more years you have to screw things up. We try to help folks understand that you've done a fantastic job of saving and climbing up that mountain, but once you've reached that peak, you've got to get down the other side. Most accidents, most injuries happen when you're going down the mountain, not up. Having that transition and becoming that spender and realizing that you've got to invest differently, is probably the most common mistake that we see our new retirees make is think.

Kevin: Okay. How do you help them with that?

Robert: A lot of it has to do with getting them to change their opinion. We could invest aggressively for them but that's not doing them any favors. There's a lot of psychology and behavioral finance that goes into a good retirement plan. I often feel like we are part investment advisor, part retirement planner, and part psychiatrist/psychologist. Getting someone to change their behavior and getting them to understand that it is okay if they make 5% when the market makes 10% because if the market loses 20%, they will not–it's a whole different mindset. We start off by just helping people realize that it's okay. We do that by doing a lot of projections that show they don't have to keep up with their aggressive behavior. They don't have to be shooting for the moon. They don't have to put their retirement dollars at risk in order to have a successful retirement.

The second part is that we try to help people understand what a successful retirement is–because it's different for everyone. It's one of the fascinating parts of our job and one of the things that we love to do is helping people figure out what a successful retirement means to them, and then how we reverse engineer it to get back to the starting point.

Kevin: Is that what you like best about your job?

Robert: It is. It's being able to go to a client and say, "You showed us what your goals are. We've figured it all out, and then we took all of these steps." I enjoy the reverse engineering process, but being able to show clients, "Look at what you have done and look at what you can do with just a little bit of tweaking and a little bit of advanced planning and preparation." You really can do so much for your future. Because, we are now living so long and retiring for so long, you have to think about 30 years out or 40 years out as you're entering into retirement. It just makes it all that much more important.

Kevin: What technique do you wish your clients knew more about? You mentioned about the mindset a minute ago.

Robert: Honestly, I wish that they understood the importance of protecting against long-term care. I wish that they understood, or took more seriously, the need for protection in retirement. With a retirement plan, you have to play offense and defense. Most clients don't want to invest the time, effort, or knowledge. They don't want to put in that work on the defensive side, which is why they hire folks like us to help them do it. I wish that they understood more the importance of protecting themselves and protecting their assets.

Kevin: Yes. I met with a guy recently who had a $400,000 investment house. We asked a lot of questions, "Do you have long-term care insurance?" He didn't. "Is your house on a trust?" It wasn't. "What's the return of investment on your equity?" He had to think for a minute and I said, "I don't mean your appreciation." He was like "I guess at zero". I said, "How do you feel about that?" He was a successful guy. That really got under his skin. You're right. People don't know what they don't know. We have to open up their minds, as it were, so they can see possibilities, so they can see options.

Robert: Yes. Intelligent, successful people get where they are because they are really good at what they do. But just because you are intelligent and successful and really good at what you do, does not mean that you are intelligent and successful and really good at all things. I think I'm an excellent retirement planner and financial planner, but if I ever have to swap out a dishwasher, our entire household might burn to the ground. We can't be good at everything. That's why it's good to know people who are good at what they do.

Kevin: Absolutely. Tell me about a recent senior client that you helped, what their situation was, what they were hoping to accomplish, and how you helped them.

Robert: I have a doctor who became my client about a year before he retired. We transferred over his assets. He wasn't happy with how things were going, how it was structured. We got things set up. At the time, he was 60. He was planning on working until 70. He had 10 years to continue funding as retirement, getting things exactly how he wanted them to be, to get to that peak of the mountain and retire. A year later, he developed a very debilitating disease. This was two years ago. At the age of 61, he had to stop working almost immediately and can never work again. But, we were able to take what he had when he came to us, what we had done and the plans that we were working on, and transition them into a plan that can keep him and his wife comfortable. We can help him through some of the struggles that they're going to be facing because of this new disability that has happened. We handle that transition from being a saver to, now, a spender.

It's now been a year that he's been retired. He is completely reliant on what he built and what he had done because he can't work again and his wife had never worked because she was a doctor's wife and a homemaker. It's been very rewarding. Unfortunately, he will probably only have about eight or 10 years because of his disease. However, his wife was about five years younger than him, she probably has 35 or 40 years left. His knowing that we've got things setup in place so that when he goes, his wife will be able to continue this lifestyle, that she will be able to stay living in the exact same house that they've been in, still doing all of the same things that they've been doing with their four children, has been very rewarding for us and very fulfilling for the doctor and his wife.

Kevin: Did they have a mortgage?

Robert: They do not have a mortgage.

Kevin: They may be candidates for a reverse because whatever their house is worth, they can get 40% of the equity in a line of credit.

Robert: How do you feel about individuals who want to pass the house on?

Kevin: This is why we love working with financial planners. Whatever equity is at stake potentially could be lost. We'd say, "Go back and talk to your financial planner." See if they qualify for an insurance policy, probably on her, and the kids end up with more money and in the long run, tax-free. If they need the long-term care, you tie that in as well.

Robert: With us, every life insurance policy that we now offer has built in automatic long-term care riders. I think that's becoming the standard in the industry.

Kevin: Good.

Robert: It definitely is with every policy that we offer. If it does not have it built in, we don't even offer it anymore.

Kevin: Who do you write your insurance through?

Robert: The insurance goes through American National. We are a broker on the investment side of things, but all of our life insurance goes through American National.

Kevin: Which is a very conservative company.

Robert: They are very conservative.

Kevin: Tell us, who is an ideal client for you, Robert?

Robert: Business owners, or I would say, upper middle class is my favorite to work with. We work with doctors, we work with attorneys, but I really love taking care of the middle class, because I grew up in it. I don't think that they're getting the help that they need. I don't think they have a lot of places to turn to. But that upper middle class, where they've got some disposable income or they've been really good savers is ideal. I want to work with folks who want the help. Folks who know they don't know, which is sometimes hard to know that you don't know. My very favorite client is a very successful doctor here in town. What I love most about him is, he is far more intelligent than me on the medical side of things. But, he realizes that I am more intelligent than him on the financial side of things and that's the way it should work. He's busy being a doctor. I'm busy doing finance. Those clients who want the help, really, are my favorite people to work with.

Kevin: What's the first step you want them to take, usually?

Robert: As far as working with us, we love to have a "get to know you" session. Honestly, we're not the right fit for everybody, and not everyone is the right fit for us. We enjoy getting to sit down with folks and find out if we match, if we have a connection, if we have similar philosophies that everybody can live with. Because you might have a wonderful person sitting in front of you that is just not going to go along with you or has the opposite opinion on absolutely everything. They're just not a right fit.

Kevin: Yes.

Robert: Really, the very first thing to do is pick up the phone and call or do some video conferencing or sit down face to face and find out "Do we fit well together?"

Kevin: Okay. How do they normally find you? Or how do you find them?

Robert: We just have educational events throughout the year. Our clients will invite other folks too, or we will open it up to the public, send out some invitations. But, for the most part, we've been about 95% to 98% referral business for the last decade.

Kevin: Wow.

Robert: We don't go looking for very many clients. It doesn't mean that we don't want to help more folks. We just don't want to go looking for them. We're planning on doing more educational events in the future. I'm probably like most financial people and enjoy speaking and love talking to as many people who will listen. I really have a good time teaching classes and doing educational seminars and workshops and events. We do host Social Security workshops, "How to invest now that you're retired" workshops. We do different educational events throughout the year.

Kevin: Awesome. Okay. As far as challenges you're facing, what's your biggest challenge right now?

Robert: I would say, because the market has been doing well for the past seven, eight years, even though we've had a little bit of stalls here and there, people tend to forget that it could go wrong again. When things are going wrong, they forget that they could ever go right again. Now that things are going right, it's harder, now, to keep people on track with protecting their assets. Everyone is in growth mode, but it's a good problem to have when the markets are growing.

Kevin: This is the second longest bull market that we've had right now?

Robert: It's the second longest bull market we've ever had. Now, everyone thinks that it's never going to end.

Kevin: Happy days are here again.

Robert: That's right.

Kevin: You mentioned the seminars. Anything else you're doing to attract new business?

Robert: The short answer is no. Referrals and educational events, that's all we do.

Kevin: What's the best advice you've ever received?

Robert: I think the best advice is to always treat your client like they're your mother. Don't do anything for your client or to your client that you would not do for or to your mother. That really helps keep us on track. It goes back to the golden rule, treat others as we would ourselves, but sometimes we don't even treat ourselves all that great, but we always take care of our moms.

Kevin: Yes. What's the best financial advice?

Robert: It's the same advice that I give my kids, "give 10, save 10, invest 10." So, 10%, 10%, 10% and then don't feel guilty about spending the rest. If you're saving, and you're investing even if the other money you spend goes wrong, you're still going to have a good future ahead of you.

Kevin: Amen to that. What would you like to share that I haven't asked you?

Robert: I would say, it's never too late to plan for your retirement. It's never too early to plan for your retirement. You can always start even if you forgot to, even if you didn't get around to it, and you should always start as soon as you possibly can when it comes to planning.

Kevin: We tell people that about mortgages. Your industry is known for telling people, "Start in your 20s as soon as you can," because you can never get that decade back. Same thing is true with the reverse mortgage. Start at 62 or as early as you can because that 5% a year, compound interest growth on one credit, you lose that decade of the 60s. You just lost eight years.

Robert: Right.

Kevin: How can people get ahold of you? What's your contact info?

Robert: They can go to the website robertedgin.com. They can call us at the office at 719-685-8585.

Kevin: That's an easy number.

Robert: It is an easy number.

Kevin: All right. Thank you so much.

Robert: Absolutely.

CHAPTER 7

Marcia Williams

Marcia Williams, CLTC, LUTCF is the founder and owner of Shiloh Insurance Solutions in Colorado Springs. She has been a licensed insurance agent since 1988. As an insurance advisor and education specialist, Marcia helps seniors coordinate their resources and assets with the appropriate Medicare Supplement and/or long-term care planning solution. She has served on the boards of numerous nonprofit organizations. Marcia and her husband have two children and eight grandchildren.

Kevin: I'm with Marcia Williams, who does Medicare planning for seniors. Marcia, what's the name of your company?

Marcia: Shiloh Insurance Solutions, LLC

Kevin: We're going to start with some background questions. Where are you from? Where did you grow up?

Marcia: I was born in Kansas, lived there six months of my life. Since my father was in the oil industry, we moved to several of the ports of call in that industry. However, I have lived in Colorado Springs since 1969.

Kevin: Oh, long time, okay. So, what was your childhood like?

Marcia: It was great. Although we did move to various locations, I enjoyed change. Because I enjoy meeting new people, it was not difficult for me. So, for me, that was fun.

Kevin: Awesome. Tell us how long you have been in the insurance business and how you got to this point in your career?

Marcia: In 1988, I began working in the insurance business focusing on life and disability insurance. Approximately ten years ago, I started focusing on long-term care planning. Eventually, I began to work with people who are either currently on, or, aging into Medicare to help them determine which Medicare Insurance solutions best meet their needs.

Kevin: So, what made you want to focus on Medicare Insurance?

Marcia: I met a gentleman at a fundraiser and he was working in that particular marketplace and introduced me to a company that had relationships with many of the companies that offer Medicare Insurance. So, I got interested in that type of planning for people and contracted with several companies that provide this product. Also, I am contracted with a company in Chicago that focuses on Medicare Insurance products. In addition to my Colorado clients, I also work with those in Illinois, New Mexico, Oklahoma and Texas.

Kevin: So, what do you wish you knew when you started that you now know?

Marcia: Some years ago, I met a woman that sold Medicare Insurance. However, I had no understanding of it because I did not even know what Medicare was at that point. As the years went along, I began to understand the significant number of people aging into Medicare every day. So, it became apparent there was need to understand the issues surrounding Medicare and Medicare insurance in order to help educate those who were being affected by Medicare. Yet, what I discovered is many people have no idea about Medicare and the Medicare Insurance planning they must make. Actually, I would say 99.99% of people really don't have any idea when they get to this age. They're very confused, and most people are very honest about their confusion. Every so often I meet someone who thinks they understand and then they talk to me a year or so later having made some decisions that will cost them penalties because they have not met some of the major deadlines which must be met regarding Medicare and Medicare Insurance.

Kevin: It's a little overwhelming for our seniors.

Marcia: It's absolutely overwhelming. I even have clients with multiple or advanced degrees that tell me they "just don't get this stuff". The people I talk with who are candid about their confusion are very willing to receive advice because they find this transition into Medicare so overwhelming.

Kevin: So why is it so complicated?

Marcia: I used to think age 65 was old. Of course, I no longer think that as I have aged. It seems at this point in their lives, most people want things to be a bit easier. Often, the have been insured under a group insurance or individual insurance plan and understand how those work. But, this is totally different. There are deadlines you have to meet, there are many rules associated with Medicare planning, Medicare insurance, Medicare Advantage Plans, or prescription drug plans known as Part D. So, it's just a lot of navigation and decision making that must be made in a very short period of time.

Kevin: Marcia, what are the highlights of your position? What do you enjoy most about what you do?

Marcia: Working and building relationships with those I serve. Hearing them share things they probably wouldn't tell anybody else because they trust me. Just enjoying people and getting to know them and understanding their story. And, being able to help them make a good decision based on their needs, and with the options available to them.

Kevin: When did you start Shiloh Insurance?

Marcia: Shiloh Insurance Solutions, LLC was organized in 2008.

Kevin: So, one of the big things for seniors is their independence and wanting to stay in their homes as long as they can. With what you do, how do you help them to do that?

Marcia: Well, I provide them possible solutions to their Medicare Insurance needs then help them determine their best option in terms of their Medicare insurance needs taking into consideration their need for medical insurance balanced with their ability to pay premiums short-range and long-range that will affect their financial stability.

Since there are 10 different plans, sometimes the most cost-effective plan may not always be the cheapest premium. So, we have to look at their particular needs not only currently, but also look at potential obstacles down the road. Some of these decisions have long-lasting financial consequences and some cannot be re-made without serious repercussions to their financial health.

Kevin: So, when you say there are all these different plans, is it such that you have healthy people that rarely go to the doctor and then you've got people that are at the doctor every week? Is that the range of plans or is it more we have X number of prescriptions and we need this or whatever?

Marcia: There are several issues that must be addressed during the Medicare Insurance planning process. First, we look at whether they or spouse are currently working and have access to an Employer group health insurance plan. Then we determine if that Employer group plan has *creditable drug coverage* or if the client will have any other *creditable prescription drug coverage* available. If not, whether still under an Employer Medical Plan or a Medicare Insurance plan, a Part D plan needs to be chosen to avoid any penalties. The Part D Rx plan they choose will be based on the current medications they are taking.

Kevin: And then the plans change every year as well?

Marcia: Under current law, each year during the (AEP) annual enrollment period between October 15th and December 7th, a current Medicare insured can change their Part D Rx plan or Medicare Advantage Plan (Part

C) if needed. The new plan would then become effective on January 1 of the following year.

The drug plans do change each year based on the Medicare rules set by the (CMS) Centers for Medicare & Medicaid Services. The insurance companies must design within the constraints of these rules and have their plans approved by CMS. However, the companies do have some flexibility in their plan designs and may look different from other companies while still complying with all the CMS rules.

Kevin: And then can you have the Part D, the prescriptions with one company and the Part A with another company?

Marcia: Yes, let me clarify one thing you've said, the Part D. You can have that with any company that offers them in your state. Medicare supplements can be with any company that offer them in your zip code area but can be used anywhere in the country as long as the provider accepts Medicare and the treatment you are receiving is approved under either Medicare Part A or Part B.

Kevin: So, for people who may not be aware, why don't you just break down the different parts of Medicare: A, B and D.

Marcia: Medicare Part A covers some of the costs of hospitalization. Most people who paid into the Social Security System at least 10 years, get Medicare Part A free. If a person either did not work in the Social Security system, or did not have a spouse that did, then they will pay considerably more for Part A. Part B covers some of the doctor's and outpatient costs.

Medicare recipients pay for Part B. Approximately 95% of the recipients will pay whatever their standard Part B premium is in a given year. Although, Part B premiums can change from year to year. Additionally, those in higher income brackets may pay more for their Part B premium. According to the Medicare.gov website:

"If: Your modified adjusted gross income as reported on your IRS tax return from 2 years ago is above a certain amount. If so, you'll pay the standard premium amount and an Income Related Monthly Adjustment Amount (IRMAA). IRMAA is an extra charge added to your premium."

Kevin: So, the more you earn, the more you pay?

Marcia: Yes, I call it a *success penalty*.

Kevin: And then the Part D is for the prescriptions?

Marcia: Yes. Also, the IRMAA can be applied to Part D plans as follows from the Medicare.gov Website:

"If your income is above a certain limit, you'll pay an income-related monthly adjustment amount in addition to your plan premium".

Kevin: And the Part C is the combination of all of it?

Marcia: There are plans called Medicare Advantage (MA Part C Plans) that are a combination of Part A and B. Some MA plans also offer the Part D Rx coverage and are known as Part C MAPD plans. The MA and MAPD plans typically require the insured to use providers within a specific network. If you are allowed to go out of Network the co-pays and out of pocket maximums are often greater than in Network.

Kevin: Got it, okay.

Marcia: Also, they can have extra types of coverage outside of what is normally covered by Medicare.

Kevin: Add-ons, if you will.

Marcia: Yes. Some will offer various additional benefits such as a level of dental or vision coverage, transportation benefits, Silver Sneakers, etc. At the minimum, Part C plans must offer at least equal to what Original Medicare A and B cover.

Kevin: And somebody has to be 65 to get coverage?

Marcia: No, you just have to be on Medicare. According to Medicare.gov:

> *"If you're under 65 years old, you might be eligible for Medicare. If you receive disability benefits from Social Security or certain disability benefits from the Railroad Retirement Board (RRB) for at least 24 months in a row. If you have amyotrophic lateral sclerosis (ALS, also called Lou Gehrig's disease). If you have end-stage renal disease (ESRD). ESRD is permanent damage to the kidneys that requires regular dialysis or a kidney transplant."*

Kevin: Oh, wow, this is pretty comprehensive. So, Marcia, as seniors are aging into Medicare, what are some of the mistakes you see them make?

Marcia: A couple of things seem to be problematic. Waiting too close to the guaranteed issue deadlines for the Medicare Insurance and having to make snap decisions without thinking through the long-range ramifications of those decisions. Also, I hear about them hanging out with their buddies and friends at the club, senior center or church, etc. and one of their friends tell them: "This is what you should do because this is what I did and it is really great". What I tell my clients is the advice might be well intentioned but can have devastating consequences for them personally due to their own financial situation, health history, or medical needs

Kevin: So, let's say someone is 64. At what point should they reach out to you for help to understand what plans are available and the Medicare deadlines that must be met? Is 64 a good age or should it be sooner?

Marcia: That's a good question and age 64 would be fine. I have clients that we are able to apply for a Medicare insurance policy up to twelve months in advance of their Medicare effective date. However, each insurance company has different rules regarding how far in advance of the Medicare effective date they will accept an application. Nevertheless, I think four months out to begin a Medicare Insurance planning discussion would be the latest I would recommend.

Kevin: Okay.

Marcia: If a person is on Social Security prior to age 65, Social Security will automatically send their Medicare Card in the mail. It will have both A and B on it if recipient is eligible for both. If they are still employed and have health insurance through an active employer group, they can delay signing up for Part B without penalty if they want to stay on the group plan. If Social Security has sent them their Medicare card, they will have to notify Social Security they are delaying Part B because of current employment with group insurance. Otherwise, to avoid a late enrollment penalty and a delay in coverage, a person must sign up for Medicare within three months before the month they turn 65, the month they turn 65, or within three months of the month they turn 65.

Kevin: So, we were talking about the mistakes that you see seniors make. How do you help them solve these problems?

Marcia: It's very important they talk with someone who is an educational specialist with Medicare Insurance planning well in advance of the deadlines they must meet in order to make timely decisions. Someone who can help them review their options and help them determine what is best for their personal situation. Also, someone to explain the late enrollment penalties they will face if they don't have Part B or Part D drug coverage in place by the Medicare timelines.

Kevin: Okay.

Marcia: They could be depending on the person's situation, but not automatically.

Kevin: So, you could go on Medicare without taking Social Security?

Marcia: Yes. They can be decisions independent of each other based on a person's needs and the Medicare rules of which they are subject in their particular situation.

Kevin: Okay. Who are the different providers out there that offer Medicare policies?

Marcia: Dozens and dozens.

Kevin: Not just a few?

Marcia: No, many, many companies.

Kevin: Wow. What do you like best about your business, Marcia?

Marcia: I like the fact that I am helping people. Plus, the experience I bring to the equation since I've experienced this process through caring for elderly family members, clients, and personal planning decisions. So I have a personal knowledge of how these decisions can affect people in various situations and life stages. In the end, I enjoy helping people find the best solutions to their needs not my needs or someone else's. I've built my business on the Golden Rule; doing for others what I would do for myself in a similar situation.

Kevin: What product or technique or service do you offer that you wish more senior clients knew about?

Marcia: Well, in terms of what I do, I'm very detail oriented and really try to explain the whole scenario to them in terms of their situation and how it fits into what the Medicare rules are; to help them become totally informed. A sidebar is I think a lot of people are just getting into the industry, or they're not very cautious, and they're not explaining everything the person needs to know. Typically, when I talk to someone that's already been in contact with another insurance agent, it becomes apparent they have not been educated as thoroughly as needed to make an informed decision about this planning decision. Often, I am complimented because I have been thorough and provided them with information and resources of which they were unaware. So that leads me to believe there are people out there that are not disclosing all the information needed for a person to truly make an informed decision.

Kevin: So, tell us about a recent client. We don't want to hear any names or anything, but what was their situation specifically as a senior that you help with these kinds of issues? What were they hoping to accomplish, and how did you help them?

Marcia: Oh, wow! I speak with dozens of people each month. But, I think the key to what I just mentioned can be described in the following situation. I spoke with a lady this week that thought she had it all figured out. She had been talking with lots of people. Which, incidentally, gets very confusing for people. But it was really clear in the conversation that there were some major pieces of the Medicare Insurance picture she had not been given. So, I was able to share some points with her that made a big difference in her planning decision. Had she made a different decision without the full facts needed to make an informed decision, there could have been serious consequences in her situation. So, she was extremely thankful for me taking the time to thoroughly inform her and help her make the best Medicare Insurance decision that would meet her needs.

Kevin: Absolutely. So, with the Medicare providers you work with, are there some that are stock companies, and some that are mutual companies? In other words, the members own the company, the mutual company or the stock, and the stockholders own the companies.

Marcia: Yes, there are both stock and mutual companies in the Medicare Insurance market. One of the larger carriers I work with is a major player in this industry. In fact, they are the largest customer-owned insurer in the country.

Kevin: Interesting, wow. Marcia, who's an ideal client for you?

Marcia: An ideal client would be someone who is just aging into Medicare or just getting on Medicare because of a health issue. Someone who desires help to understand their Medicare Insurance options. Someone who will allow me to listen to their needs, and explain their options, and answer their questions. Also, to allow me to explain the Medicare and Medicare Insurance deadlines as it applies to their particular situation and the penalties associated with those deadlines.

Kevin: What's the first step you want these ideal clients to take?

Marcia: To contact me or someone who has experience with the Medicare rules surrounding Medicare Insurance planning and can explain the different parts to Medicare. Also, someone who will review their insurance options, the time frames insurance can be applied for and put into place to avoid penalties or perhaps the inability to apply for a Medicare Insurance policy.

Kevin: And how do your ideal clients usually find you?

Marcia: In Colorado, I work with referrals and in the other states where I am licensed, the Agency through which I am associated provides many referrals and leads.

Kevin: I see. And how do you market your services to your potential ideal clients to make them aware of you?

Marcia: Well, right now, most of my Colorado clients come from referrals or know of me and reach out to me personally. The Agency I subcontract with in Chicago does major marketing in four states. So, I have clients in multiple states who have reached out to us for help because the carrier we represent is very well known and has been in the marketplace a very long time. I also get referrals from my clients in other states. Additionally, we get a high direct mail response so we can also reach out to those people who contact us. When we have time (not often) we can do cold calling to some of the 10,000 per day who are turning 65 in our country!

Kevin: So, tell us this, this company that you write a lot of business with that you said is very well known, who is it?

Marcia: In Illinois, Oklahoma, Texas, and New Mexico, I write exclusively with Blue Cross Blue Shield because they are a major player in the Health Insurance market in those states and are very well known and trusted. In Colorado, I will typically quote among the five major companies I feel are most competitive premium-wise and have proven themselves by providing timely Medicare Insurance claims processing and great customer service in our state.

Kevin: What's the biggest challenge you're facing right now?

Marcia: I think the biggest challenge is having the time to meet the needs of the large number of people that are aging into Medicare on a daily basis. Also, making sure we can somehow be in contact with as many of those people as possible who want help in order to provide resources and planning tools which will help them decide and determine what's best for their particular situation.

Kevin: What's the best advice you've ever received?

Marcia: Well, from an insurance standpoint, it has always been about fact finding. Finding out what the client wants and needs. This is about them, not me. With that thought in mind, I will recommend to them what I would do for myself in a similar situation with all things being equal. So, I think that's the critical piece.

Kevin: What would you like to share that I haven't asked you?

Marcia: You have been very thorough and thoughtful with your questions. So, for me to reiterate, I would say the most important piece of a person's Medicare and Medicare Insurance planning is to be thinking of the issues well in advance of the decision-making deadlines. We mentioned earlier perhaps even a year in advance. Start thinking through, "Am I going to be retiring when I turn 65? Am I going to wait until I'm 66? Do I have health insurance through my employer right now? Do I have it as an individual? Even if I have it through my employer, is it going to be less expensive to get an individual Medicare supplement and a prescription drug plan?"

Kevin: So, with a couple, the man turns 65, the wife isn't 65 yet, she has to wait?

Marcia: That's correct. Medicare is individual so it's based on an individual's eligibility for Medicare. Let's say John was working at ABC Company and Mary is covered under his group health insurance plan. He is now 65 and has decided he wants to retire and go on Medicare. He knows he's not going to be able to keep his group insurance even if he wants to when he retires. Very seldom will a group insurance plan let family members stay on a group insurance plan when the primary insured is no longer covered. Now what will Mary do for insurance? She could get COBRA for 18 months, then still have to get an individual insurance policy until she turns 65. Or, perhaps she is also employed and can change her insurance coverage to her employer plan. If John worked for a company that would allow him to stay on a retirement insurance plan at retirement, he might choose to do so in order to provide health insurance for Mary until she turns 65. In that case he would have to factor in the cost of paying the government for his Part B Medicare insurance premium along with his group insurance premium.

In that scenario, John might find it more cost effective to purchase a Medicare Supplement for himself and find an individual insurance plan for Mary. This is a great example of the need to have someone walk through all of your options to help determine which is most cost effective.

As a reminder, when a Medicare eligible individual turns 65 and is no longer actively working, they must sign up for Medicare even if they are insured under a retirement plan.

Kevin: How can people reach you or learn more about you?

Marcia: Email or phone. My business phone is 719-694-3966. They can reach me at marcia@shilohsolutions.com.

Kevin: Thank you, Marcia.

CHAPTER 8

Cavin Harper

Cavin Harper is the founder and president of the Christian Grandparenting Network, based in Colorado Springs, which helps both individuals and churches across the country strengthen the grandparent-grandchild bond.

He is the author of three books, *Courageous Grandparenting: Unshakable Faith in a Broken World*, *Living your Will*, and *Wayfinder: Keeping Faith in a Shattered World*. Cavin and his wife Diane are also the creators of *GrandCamps*, where grandparents and grandchildren build memories that last a lifetime.

Cavin and Diane and have been married since 1969. They have two daughters and nine grandchildren.

Kevin: I'm with Cavin Harper. He's the founder of the Christian Grandparenting Network. Thanks for taking some time to be interviewed today, Cavin.

Cavin: My pleasure.

Kevin: So tell us, where are you from? Where did you grow up?

Cavin: I grew up in Cheyenne, Wyoming. Was born in Waco, Texas while my dad was attending Baylor University. So, while I was still an infant, moved back to Cheyenne and that's where I grew up.

Kevin: Awesome. Tell us about your childhood. What was that like?

Cavin: I'm the oldest of six children so there was always lot going on in our home. Cheyenne was a great place to grow up. It was a small enough community that you felt like you knew a lot of people. Unlike today, when I was in grade school and junior high, Mom just said, "Hey, just let me know. You need to be back here by suppertime. Tell me where you're going but you just need to be here for suppertime." And we were all over town. We never had to worry about anything. So it was really one of those carefree kinds of experiences growing up in my childhood. We were always out in the streets playing or out in the prairie or riding our bikes across town collecting pop cans or pop bottles. Getting some spending money. So it was a lot of fun.

We grew up in a church environment as well. And so that was a major part of my childhood. Being involved in activities of the church. Sitting on the front row of church every week as my dad led the singing and directed the choir.

Kevin: All right.

Cavin: And kept an eye on us.

Kevin: I bet.

Cavin: It was a good time. We didn't move around a lot. We only lived in two houses during my entire time growing up. Most of those years were in one house that my wife and I ended up buying from my dad when we got married.

Kevin: Okay.

Cavin: We always had that stability. We always knew where home was.

Kevin: Tell us about your parents. What did they do?

Cavin: Mom was a housewife. She had six kids to take care of so that was full-time. Dad was a business entrepreneur. He had his own business in household goods moving an agent for North American Van Lines. He also had a crane and heavy hauling service, self-storage, carpet cleaning.

Kevin: Oh wow.

Cavin: And... Sand blasting. You name it, he was dabbling in it.

Kevin: Quite the entrepreneur.

Cavin: Yeah.

Kevin: So you've had a career before you started Christian Grandparenting Network. Tell us a little bit of your background.

Cavin: Well, when I got out of college I thought I was going to work with someone like Youth for Christ. That was really my dream, to do that. Some things changed before I graduated and I realized that it probably wasn't the direction I wanted to go. So I went to work with my dad for the first five and a half years after college. Worked in the business, helped get the self storage business started and worked my way up in the company. He made me start out doing grunt work doing the heavy stuff -- moving furniture, learning to pack and all that kind of stuff. So I worked in the warehouse until I got a little experience, and then moved into the office.

After that, then, I really still felt that need and call to go into church ministry and a couple of the staff people at my church were constantly encouraging me to do that. So I left the business and went to seminary. I graduated from seminary in 1977 and went straight into church work in a church in Denver where I was on staff for 17 years.

When I left the church ministry in 1992, it was to take over a retreat center west of Colorado Springs called Christ Haven Lodge that my dad had bought when he sold one of his businesses. My wife and I moved up there for what we thought was going to be a one year project getting the place fixed up enough that we could get it on the market and sell it. But we ended up staying 10 years running it, contracting with an organization that did mission training there. They now have their headquarters at Palmer Lake. We did all of their core programs and so our place was full year round. We did that for 10 years before we finally realized I still needed to sell it. But while I was there, we started what is now called Christian Grandparenting Network. Then it was called ElderQuest Ministries.

We thought initially it would be to have some extra programs for our facilitators during some of the down times. It ended up growing into this Grandparenting thing, which I am now currently doing. It all started there in 1997.

Kevin: That's awesome. Tell us more about the Christian Grandparenting Network. Who do you serve and how do you serve them? And you mentioned you have a conference coming up as well.

Cavin: Christian Grandparenting Network is intended to be a ministry that's focused on challenging and equipping grandparents to be intentional about their biblical roles. I don't think any of us would deny the fact that there's no greater joy for a parent or a grandparent than to know that their kids and their grandkids are walking in the truth. So our objective is to call grandparents to awareness that, number one, Grandparenting is important to God because he has a lot to say about it in scripture. I didn't know that, frankly, before but he has a lot to say about it. And number two, that for our new grandparents to understand that you can't give what you don't have. So if you're going to be giving a legacy to your grandchildren that really matters for eternity, you better make sure that your life lines up with that reality.

So we're there to challenge grandparents to that awareness and then to the commitment to say, "I want to be intentional. What does that look like?" That's where we come in, to say, "Here's what the word of God says about what an intentional grandparent is and here are some tools and resources." So we're really about providing teaching and resources to grandparents, which is why the coalition is such an important piece. Because we began realizing that little by little we were running into people who had a similar vision to ours, that wanted to do more and felt like everybody was out there doing their thing by themselves. So we formed this coalition of people committed to that message and now we're able to provide a whole lot more resources. When we started the coalition two years ago there were only around seven resources out there that were of any real value to grandparents in terms of this intentionality piece I mentioned.

We now have probably 12 – 14 resources with another six or seven in the works. So we're all about providing those resources and encouraging grandparents to stay active in their grandkids' and their adult kids' lives but also to make sure that their lives are lined up with God's Word. I sometimes will say to grandparents, "Make sure that you're spending yourself for the next generation, not just spending on yourself." What are the assets and resources God has given you and how are you using them to further the kingdom to make sure your grandchildren have a heritage and a legacy that you want to pass on to them that will allow you to continue doing what you're doing?

Kevin: That's awesome. So Cavin, what do you wish you knew when you started that you now know?

Cavin: When I started the ministry?

Kevin: Yes.

Cavin: Good question. What would I wish that I had known? I don't know. I suppose I would say I wish I had known how challenging it really is to be the kind of grandparent I think God wants us to be in this world that we live in today. A postmodern world where families don't live together anymore. A world that says, basically, parents, those kids are your responsibilities and nobody else's. The expectation is that when my adult children grow up and leave the house and get married they live their own life, I live my own life. And so the challenge for us is, when we look at what God says about family and intentionality, I wish I'd have known a little bit more about why we are doing what we do today in our culture and how best to address that. Because, really, I can't talk to people about living the way we lived 200 years ago when families did live together. It's a little more challenging.

I think there was some naiveté on my part coming into this as to how that should flesh out. The other piece I wish I had known more when I was married was what to look forward to when children came along and how to incorporate Mom and Dad and in-laws in that picture. I never had any perspective on what that should look like myself. So I wish I'd had someone say to me, when I got married, "You know, when you start having kids, this isn't just about you."

Kevin: What are the highlights of your position?

Cavin: Oh, I suppose it's the people that I meet. The stories that I hear from people who say, "This is like an Aha moment for me. I wish somebody had told me this a long time ago. How come people aren't talking about this in the church? Why aren't people teaching us, equipping us as grandparents?" It's just the engagement with people... to hear their stories and to hear their heart and their passion once they realize how important they are and that they really can matter. I don't think there's anything more exciting to me. I mean, there are times when I say, "Lord, why do you have me doing this? I'm the least qualified person for this. I've got two prodigal grandsons. I've got family that has got all kinds of issues and problems itself.

Why am I doing this?" And then God will send people into my life, who say, "You know, I'm so grateful that you are out there speaking this message because it's changed my life. Changed my family's life."

So, for me, it's just the knowledge that I'm where God wants me to be for whatever reason God has me here. I don't know why he has me doing this. I have no clue. I have no clue. But it's just knowing that I'm here and being able to be a part of something bigger than myself that I had never dreamed of doing before.

Kevin: This is a book to help seniors. What are some of the mistakes you see seniors make as they approach or are in retirement?

Cavin: You know what the biggest one is, is that they think they've done their time and it's just time for them to go to play and enjoy Leisureville for the rest of their lives. And they forget that this is a time in their life when they are most needed. That their stories need to be heard. Their wisdom, their input needs to be received and heard. Their assets need to be employed in ways that teach their kids the value of wealth and why God has given it to us. The value of just being a steward of everything that God has given. Not just wealth and material assets but what about the lessons that I've learned in life? What about the knowledge God has given me in all these areas of life that I need to pass on to others? What about the story of my story in God's big story? I want them to understand that they're part of that story and it's the only story that's the story of real reality.

So I think the biggest mistake grandparents make is to think that they've done their time and they're no longer needed. And it's just not true. So they go and spend on themselves and waste what they have. By the way, I'm all for grandparents going and having some good times because they need to be able to get away once in a while and enjoy this time of life. But it seems to me everything Jesus told me about life is that it's about spending ourselves for the sake of those around us. And who better to be doing that than our own family? Our own grandkids?

Kevin: What are some ways you help seniors solve these problems?

Cavin: Years ago I wrote a little book thing that's kind of a workbook. It's called *Living Your Will*. Some people misunderstand the title. It's not about living my will, in other words, what I will to do. But it's taking the living will and establishing a new paradigm that says instead of a living will that says how I want to be unplugged when the time comes for that to happen, why not a new living, living will perspective that says how I want to be plugged in to use all the resources and assets God has given me for the sake of another generation. That they may know God, may know Christ, and walk in his troop.

So for me, one of the things I like to be able to do is remind grandparents, take an inventory of all the assets God has given to you. Material and non-material. What are those assets that God has given to you? Do you even recognize what you have that God's entrusted to you? Then ask this question, "God what do you want me to do with these? Who should be the beneficiary of those assets while I'm still living?" So that's one of the things I always say to grandparents. John Piper wrote a book years ago called *Don't Waste*

Your Life. We might want to say to grandparents, "Don't waste your life." One of the best ways to make sure that that doesn't happen is to understand what God has given to us and why he has given it to us and who it is he wants to bless and benefit from those things.

Kevin: This is really the legacy piece, isn't it?

Cavin: It is. You know, Proverbs 13:22 says a righteous man leaves an inheritance or a legacy or a heritage, whatever word you want to use there, for his children's children. And I think it is. And I just want grandparents to think of it in terms of everything. Not just your portfolio, but what is your story? What has God shown you about his glory, his grace and his goodness that the next generation needs to know? How can I help my grandchildren understand that they are valued not by what they do but who they are? A child of God made in his image. And in that there is joy, there's value, there's meaning, there's purpose. I want my grandchildren to know that. I want them to know it by the way in which I live, how I am spending what God has given to me? Am I spending it only on myself?

I learned something important from my dad. He did really well at building a financial portfolio to take care of him and his wife, and I'm grateful for that because otherwise the burden would have fallen on us. But he taught me well that the resources God has given me don't belong to me. Whatever they are. They don't belong to me. So let's use them well. Let's be good stewards of those things. Let's not build bigger homes, let's build bigger rewards.

Kevin: That's awesome. What do you like best about your ministry?

Cavin: The teaching. One of the pieces that we started, one of the very first things that we did, was what we called GrandCamp for grandparents and their grade school aged grandchildren to come together for five days. Of course we had the retreat center so we started it there. And we spent that time with just Grandma and Grandpa and their grandkids. Mom and dad aren't allowed. It's just them building a relationship and exploring God's truths together. It's about how we build this legacy for this generation. How do we model for them? So one of the greatest joys for me has been a part of that exploration with all these grandparents over the last 19 years doing these programs.

I was just up at Estes Park earlier this week. One of our GrandCamps was going on and it was just fun to walk in the door and see all these grandparents exploring what it means to be intentional, good stewards but also engaging with their grandchildren in really significant ways. Not just having fun. They were having lots of that, but also being able just to share their stories and to dig into God's word with them. To say, what really is important? Why are we here? There aren't many parents that I know who have those kinds of conversations with their kids. So to be able to be a part of something like that, where they're starting to see, I really can have these conversations. And the kids care, they're interested. They really want to know. That's fun, to me.

Kevin: Is there a product or a technique or a service you offer you wish more of your senior constituents knew about?

Cavin: Interesting question. Product, service, technique. Well, we're always looking for new opportunities to explore areas of need. So that's one of the things that we are trying to build ourselves, are those kinds of resources. So what we're trying to say is, "Where are the needs?" We know, for example, there are grandparents that have special needs grandkids. So what are the needs that they have that are unique from everybody else? There are grandparents that are raising their grandkids. There are grandparents who are long distance grandparents. There are grandparents who are just saying, "Okay, so what do I do with the wealth and resources that I've accumulated? How can I pass those on to the next generation? What's the best way to do that?" Because I don't want them to be just a silver spoon kind of thing.

If we're talking to grandparents about using their assets well, I think one of the products that we need to explore that we haven't is, "How do you deal with your assets? What are God's expectations for you in using your assets well as a steward of those assets? The Parable of the Talents." So that's an important piece. Building your estate. Managing that estate. Making sure that that estate is used wisely. I think I'd write a book how not to spend on yourself but to spend yourself wisely for others.

Kevin: Tell us about somebody recently that you've worked with, we don't want to know their name or anything like that, but a senior with an interesting or unique situation. What were they hoping to accomplish and how did you help them?

Cavin: I get a lot of e-mails from people who are struggling with relationships with their adult children. And that's probably the most common thing I get. Adult children that are antagonistic to their values and beliefs or just have strained relationships. Or who don't want them talking to their grandchildren about God and faith. Or just, it's our job to raise our kids, stay out of it. Some of them are really, really sad stories. Tragic stories. Some are just hard. And so I think of a woman that just recently made contact and said, "I don't really know what to do. I've got a daughter who doesn't want to have anything to do with me anymore and she's just doing stupid things and my granddaughter's paying the price for her stupidity. Now she won't let me be around her either. What do I do?"

And I think, for me, it was just being able to talk to her a little bit about being authentic and honest about yourself. Instead of looking at your daughter and saying, "Look at all these terrible things that she's doing," ask yourself the question "Why is she doing it? Is there something in you that may be causing her to do what she's doing? If she's saying she wants nothing to do with you, why do you think that is? And to be able to help her stop at least, I don't know what she did with it, but to say, "You know, you're right. Maybe I've been looking at the wrong person. I need to look at me and ask myself, how am I coming across to my daughter? What are the barriers and the obstacles I'm putting up? Would she say that I'm humble or do I always have to be right?" I don't know what she did with this. But it was good to hear her say, "I never thought about those things before."

Kevin: Tell us about the type of person and the type of couple, or family, that is ideal for Christian Grandparenting Network.

Cavin: I don't think there is such a thing.

Kevin: So you can help anybody from any walk of life, any background?

Cavin: I don't know if I can help them but I can at least point them to resources or people who, perhaps, can. I think we want to be able to say there's no one size fits all kind of approach for anything in life. And that's especially true in Grandparenting. But, you know what? Even if we're coming from similar situations like, "Here's a whole group of people who are raising their grandkids full-time." There's similarity but there are a whole lot of different and unique situations in each of those stories. So to come in and say "Well, you just have to do this, this and this and that's going to solve your problem" is ridiculous. So what we want to be able to say is, "We don't care what your story is, what your situation is, if you're a grandparent and you want to matter for the things that matter in your grandkids lives, let's talk."

Kevin: How do people find out about your ministry now?

Cavin: Oh, that's a good question. Social media. Word of mouth mostly. GrandCamp ministries that we do through the Legacy Coalition. I do 10-12 seminars a year around the country and so every time I do one of those it's exposure to more people who then call and say, "Hey, I'd like to do this here. Can we do it?" Or, "Hey, I never knew there was a GrandCamp. I'm all about that."

Kevin: You do them all over the country?

Cavin: The GrandCamps or the seminars?

Kevin: GrandCamps.

Cavin: GrandCamps. Right now we have four. Colorado, South Carolina, New York and Minnesota. Next year we're hoping to have Canada, Oregon, Washington, Texas and maybe California.

Kevin: That's awesome. What would you say the biggest challenge you're facing right now with your ministry?

Cavin: Money. Everybody loves what we're doing but we haven't found that way of tugging at people's hearts enough that they want to release some of their financial resource to help us keep going. That's just been a struggle. I mean, we have all kinds of people who say. "I love what you're doing, thank you for the books" and all this kind of stuff. So the books help but when we say you know, for us to continue this new project that we need to do we need $10,000 to make it happen, it just doesn't seem to come in. So that's always been a big issue. How do we more effectively connect people that way? Most of our donors are people who have been in our GrandCamp.

Kevin: Sure. I bet. They've tasted and seen.

Cavin: Yep.

Kevin: Cavin, what's the best advice you've ever received?

Cavin: I suppose one of them was truth is always strong even though it may appear to be weak and irrelevant. But falsehood is always weak even if it appears strong and relevant. So make sure that you know the difference between what's true and what's not.

Kevin: What would you like to share that I haven't already asked you?

Cavin: Just that somehow the people that you're talking to would understand that their life isn't over, it may have just begun. And to not let society dictate their value. To understand that their value is in who they are, God's made them. And God isn't done with them. God has given them opportunities they may not have even yet realized. Go for those opportunities. Stay involved. Make sure that what you stay involved in really matters for another generation. For eternity. But stay involved. You matter. I want them to know they matter and they matter to God, they matter to their families, they matter to society. Even though they don't always know that. But they do. So don't run off and just retreat and play. Be like Caleb who said, "I'm ready and as vigorous now as I was at 40. Give me the hill country."

Kevin: Yeah. That's a great example. Where can our readers go to learn more about Christian Grandparenting Network?

Cavin: Christiangrandparenting.net.

Kevin: Thank you very much, Cavin.

Cavin: Thank you, Kevin.

CHAPTER 9

Tom Rasmussen

Tom Rasmussen is president of Clear Solutions Insurance Services in Colorado Springs. He has helped thousands of people across the country with life, disability and long-term care planning.

Tom has published articles for industry magazines and local newspapers, and been interviewed numerous times on radio regarding senior issues and the importance of income protection planning. He also co-hosts the streaming TV show on the ASY network, *New Horizons: Living Life to the Fullest*, focusing on seniors getting the most out of their lives.

Tom is a member of the non-profit LTC Forum Panel of Colorado, which advises state legislators and industry experts on long-term care planning issues. He provides education seminars and workshops to many senior and pre-retirement groups throughout the state.

Tom also enjoys hiking, completing two 14'ers and the Manitou Incline twice in 2016, along with biking the many beautiful trails around and through Colorado Springs, and spending time with his wife, children, and grandchildren.

Kevin: Tom, tell us where you grew up?

Tom: I had a normal childhood growing up, living life large

in Southern California. My parents moved up to Northern California when I was a sophomore in high school. That was a bit of an adjustment, changing high schools in the middle of sophomore year.

In 1976, I went to work in the retail record business with eventually moved back to southern California. After several years in the record industry I became a buyer for one of the largest record chains in CA, Music Plus. I spent nine years of my life working in the record business, but in 1985 I decided to move back to Northern California and join my father in the insurance business.

Kevin: Is that what he did for a living?

Tom: He was in the insurance business, but he didn't do what I do now. At the time, he represented banks that offered credit life and disability for consumer loans. He also dealt with force-placed collateral. That is when you take out a loan for a car or a home, and you didn't provide insurance, the bank would force-place it. That's how I got into the insurance business with my father.

He had many independent banks up and down the state of California and we did that together for probably two-and-a-half years, traveling the state of California working with banks with those two products.

Then my dad retired and, as things go, change came to the banking insurance business. Banks quit doing consumer loans and started getting more into commercial and real estate. Credit unions took over the consumer lending, and car dealerships started doing their own financing. So, I realized if I didn't make a change, this was going to be a short-lived career. Banks starting to get into non-traditional insurance products like annuities, life and long-term care insurance. So, I started brokering annuities, life insurance, and long-term care. After some time, I got tired of working with banks and started recruiting agents becoming a wholesaler of annuities, life and long-term care insurance in about 14 states. I eventually sold my bank business and went into full-time brokerage.

I built up my agency to about 200 or 300 agents across the country doing nicely until 2008 and 2009 came along. With the collapse of the economy also came the collapse of my agency. Suddenly, sales decreased because no one had money to invest in their future because the economy was collapsing all over the country, but especially in CA.

I laid off my staff, and went back to personal production. I have been doing it ever since, because that's what I enjoy most. And I've been doing that for over 32 years.

Kevin: And specifically, you do income protection, so help us understand what that is.

Tom: It's basically focusing on the things that protect one's income. That's life insurance planning, long-term care planning, and disability planning. I focus on things that protect that income stream.

Kevin: So, everybody understands life insurance. You protect your income if you die. Why disability insurance?

Tom: When you look at the ratios of things happening in one's lifetime. Most people will protect their home; their car and their toys. Now the possibility of your home burning is one in 1,200, the possibility of having a total car accident is one in 480, even a major health condition, which is a constant is one in 280. But when we look at the "life Happens" events like disability, the chance is one in 25 that you will have a six-months or longer of disability in your life based on occupation. So, the question becomes "If I can't work, where's my income going to be coming from?" And then you may have medical bills on top of that. That's why disability is important to consider.

When it comes to long-term care, if you're 65 or older, it's a one in five possibility of having six months or longer a need for care. And then death is 100%.

But, those three things that I've chosen to help people understand and protect, are the three things that people generally say, "I'm going to gamble on those."

Kevin: They feel it's optional.

Tom: It is optional and most men tend to look at this differently than women. Men have tendency to convince themselves that "It's not going to happen to me." And that could be true except for death. But that is only one part of the equation. The other part of the equation is the consequence to the family. So, the actual percentage that a "Life Happens" event may occur is based on stories and excuses one might tell themselves, but if a "Life Happens" event does occur, the consequence is 100% to the family. So now one must ask themselves, are they willing to gamble with their loved one's future by burying their head in the sand and pretending that it will never happen?

That's what I'm trying to break through. This is not about buying insurance; this is about having a plan.

Kevin: So, unpack a little bit more of the long-term care insurance. What is it, why do people need it, how do they use it, and what's the best time to get it?

Tom: Right now, long-term care is one of the most misunderstood topics out there when it comes to protection because most people don't want to talk about it. When you talk about long-term care, the visual is somebody sitting in a nursing home in a wheelchair by themselves in a hallway, drooling on themselves. That's the picture that's been painted over the years. Basically, it's a sentence to die. I'm on a mission to change that perception. Just because someone needs long-term, is not a death sentence.

What makes it an overwhelming experience is not having the proper environment, support, or funding to give that person in need of care the best circumstances to thrive no matter what their condition is. That person might need a little help with day-to-day situations, to continue to live life to the fullest. That's where the disconnect comes from.

There are three people that I've dealt with in 32 years of working in this genre of protection. There are the hands-on and have tasted, touch and felt the experience up front and personal. When I'm doing seminars and workshops, because I've have had this experience with my own parents, the attendees that have had this same experience all are nodding their heads, and we connect because they've been there. They understand completely what I'm talking about.

Then there are the long-distance people. "Gee that's sad. Poor Uncle Joe, but it's never going to happen to us." They're not there on the day-to-day, so they have no idea what that looks like.

Then you have the people that never tasted it, never understood it, and they have no idea what a long-term care experience is. When I sit down with these people and go through an analysis, explaining the cost of care, they fall out of their chairs. They have no idea how expensive care is.

Kevin: So today, for example, in Colorado Springs, if somebody were to go into an assisted-living care, what would be the price range per month?

Tom: Let's go from moderate care to extreme care. If we gradually went into a caregiving situation, where we needed somebody to help us out an hour or two, three days a week, an in-home care situation, to even assisted living, you're looking at possibly $3,000 to $5,000 per month.

If it gets to the point where you now start needing 24/7 care, it can be $8,000 to $10,000-plus per month.

Kevin: I saw a statistic recently: 7% of people have long-term care, 70% are going to need some form of long-term care. Is that accurate?

Tom: Those are the numbers. Anybody can debate numbers because they don't understand where they come from.

Statistically people, 65 or older, there is a 40% to 45% chance of needing care.

I've never found numbers to be a motivating factor because it's more of an emotional situation. In every workshop and seminar, I've ever done, nobody will dispute when simply say, "The older we get, the higher the percentage of probability that we're going to need care at some point in our lives."

So as far as percentages, the point is: The longer we live, the higher percentage that there's going to be some type of life event that we're going to have to face. And, it's going to cost x amount of dollars. So, when do we put that protection plan in place?

That's where I come in, but not as a salesman. This is not about selling insurance; this is about being an advisor. They get to have a specialist that can walk each individual or couple through the scenario of, "Do you have protection? Here are your options. Let's pick one and let's find something that's going to give you peace of mind."

The thing is, people don't know what they don't know. So, if they know anything about long-term care, they probably only know about "traditional long-term care coverage." And yet, that is a fading animal, quite frankly, in this industry.

There is always the thought, "What if I never need it? I've paid all this money for nothing." My response is, "What if your home never burns down? Are you mad because somebody didn't set it on fire so you could get something out of your home insurance? Are you mad because you didn't total your car in-order to use your auto insurance?"

I'm sure you probably look at your premium every month for your auto insurance and say, "Why is it so expensive?" But, when you watch the news. What do we hear every time when these types of situations happen in one's life? The first thing in our mind is, "Thank God I have insurance." That's what insurance is for.

One of the simple things that I use in groups to understand the importance of preparing for unexpected death, a long-term care experience, or a disability, is what I call the Blank Calendar-Three-Pen exercise. I give people blank calendars, and three pens: a red, a green, and a blue pen. I ask them to write on the calendar in red all their expenses for the month. And you can imagine that most people's calendars, when they're done with that month, if they're honest with themselves, have got pretty much a good red representation.

Then, I ask them to write in the green pen when the money flows in. If it's a couple, they write down, "Get paid here, the 1st or 5th, what have you." And then, bam, life happens. Something happened to you. You had an accident, you're disabled, there's an unexpected death. You've got a long-term care situation that might even be attributed to disability as well. So now, you've lost income, and now you get the extra expense of caregiving.

You cross off, with the blue pen, that income stream that's interrupted by that life event. Now look at that calendar. Are you okay?"

If you can't look at that and say, "yes, I'm okay," we probably need to chat. It's about getting past the denial. My impact graphic is the guy who's got his head buried in the sand. Everyone likes to say, "It's never going to happen to me," yet, Colorado Springs care communities are springing up all over the city. If I were able to take somebody by the hand and take them through each community, I bet you everyone we talked to in those communities would tell you the same thing: it was never going to happen to them either. We have a lot of facilities filled with a lot of people that it was never going to happen to.

Kevin: That's human nature, isn't it? Yesterday, a client that I had helped last December bought a house with a reverse mortgage. Her husband had died. She came in and said, "I'm not going to have a mortgage payment, right?" I told her she would not. She said, "Good, because that's the only way I can stay in my house."

As you work specifically with seniors, what are some highlights that light your fire? What encourages you, or makes you say, "That's why I do this?"

Tom: The perception of reverse mortgages being a "last chance" option has changed, much like the ever-changing marketplace. It's not just a "last chance" option anymore. We've had some great discussions about how that's become such an important financial vehicle.

It's the same thing with protection products. I can provide a life insurance policy, bundled with some type of a long-term care or chronic illness rider. The idea of never needing it and having wasted your money is becoming antiquated. If it's bundled with a life insurance product and someone happens to have a long-term care experience, they can draw from that death benefit to pay for it. And by the way, they draw from it income tax-free. If they never have that long-term care experience, at some point in time, they're going to pass away. Their heirs are going to get that death benefit, again, income tax-free.

And by the way, a lot of these newer life-combo products have exit strategies. At some point in time, you can leave it, and take your money back. Some of them even have income solutions, where if you don't die, you don't have a long-term care experience, you can start pulling from your death benefit to support your income.

Where's the downside here? You're basically putting money in place that will be paid out at some place. Every time I bring this up to people, they don't know it exists. So, that's my point: we don't know what we don't know. When I sit down with people that immediately say "I know you can't do anything for me," or, "I can't afford this," or "I'm too old," If they allow me the opportunity to do the research, a lot of time I can come up with something and they will say, "I never knew that I could do this."

I just did it. I'm working with an 82-year-old female today that I met at one the classes I teach in town. The first thing she did after the class was tell me, "I'm 82 years old, I'm sure you can't do anything for me." Well, we're doing something for her right now. And she was surprised that she still had an option at her age.

Kevin: What, specifically, do you say to them, or how do you help them stay in their homes? That's the number one thing they want to do, of course, is to live in their home for as long as they can.

Tom: I've got to tell you, that's not always the best situation, but you're right, most people would like to stay in their homes. I've had to change my position on that, especially being here in Colorado Springs. I've immersed myself in the care communities of this city, and I've realized that this comes back to education. People need to educate themselves on the care options that are available and to decide what's best for the person that needs the care at the time they need it.

I spent time in memory care communities and I observe the residents and I realized that a lot of these people are much better cared for in a care community than being at home. What prolongs life in many cases is engagement, a sense of involvement, being part of a community. And that can be lost if one tries to stay at home.

Kevin: They become isolated.

Tom: Staying at home in isolation and loneliness can be the kiss of death. I build funding plans to help provide choices, so one can decide what's best for the circumstances at the time. If it's at home and you've got a great support staff, great. You've got the money to do that. If it's going to an assisted-living facility, great, you've got the money to do that. If you have to go further, you've got the funding vehicle. That's what I do; I put together the funding vehicle to give you choices so you can make the right decisions that are going to help that person live life to the fullest and to the end.

Kevin: As far as financial products or tools, what do you recommend to your clients?

Tom: It depends on the situation. My first sit-down with any prospect is what I call the "introductory analysis." I don't present them with anything other than a fact-finding sheet, and I ask, "Okay, where are you at? What are your concerns? What do you have available? What don't you have available? Where are your gaps? What coverage's do you currently have, and what are your desires?"

People are so reluctant to plan for this, especially with long-term care. Everybody knows they're going to die, but as far as other scenarios the general opinion is that long-term care is one of those things that only happens to other people. Disability is one of those things as well, but, that's a reality. When I do my workshops, I make everybody close their eyes, and I walk them thorough a virtual "Life Happens' event and then I ask them to answer four questions. See if people haven't answered these four questions honestly, they have not dealt with the subject matter honestly."

The first question is: "You've just gotten into an accident; you broke both your arms and your leg. You need help. Who's going to be your caregiver?"

A typical response is: "Oh, my spouse."

"Oh, does your spouse work? Would she have to quit? Can she lift you, or vice-versa? Does she have the skillset?"

"Oh, maybe my kids."

"Are you going to move in with them, or are they going to move in with you?"

I walk them through this virtual reality so they can start seeing this, so they don't have to be unprepared if it happens. Now they start saying, "No, I'd rather have my wife supervise my care, as opposed to being my caregiver. I want to give the gift of life to my children, as opposed to asking them to put their lives on hold."

"Okay, great. Where do you want to receive your care?"

"At home."

We discuss what that looks like. I ask, "Have you ever seen some of these other facilities? Because, these are not your grandfather's nursing homes anymore." We address how much it costs and how they would pay for it. We talk about their financial position and funding. We talk about how it is going to affect their family because ultimately that's the most important consequence here.

Once we've walked through those these steps, I now have people's attention. Now they understand this is something that's important. Now we talk about the four planning elements: your savings, your government, your family, and your long-term care funding plan.

I ask what option is best suited to them. Now we can have an honest, open dialogue about how to address the things we've just gone through, from a virtual long-term care experience or a disability experience. When we find what fits their situation, then we can put a plan together that fills those gaps.

That's one of the differences, where I advise. I guide them and we get to an end-point where there's a clear understanding of what we're trying to achieve.

Kevin: What are some of the most common mistakes you see senior clients make when trying to stay in their homes?

Tom: One of the common mistakes, whether it's related to the home or not, is waiting too long. One of the biggest things they don't understand, as much as I try to explain this to people, is that this is a health-based protection option.

Kevin: Your health qualifies you.

Tom: It's so funny. When I'm in front of groups, and I ask, "How many people think money buys insurance?" I get the whole group raising their hands. Then I say, "You're all wrong!"

And they say, "What are you talking about?"

I say, "Health is what allows you to get this." You could have all the money in the world, but if you don't have good health, you don't get it.

We take the approach of, "if you want to stay at home, what does that look like? If it's moderate care, it could be this much." As much as we talk about the expense of a semi-private or private room in a care community, it's even more expensive to have 24/7 care at home. It goes back to that, "Who's going to provide it?"

In Colorado Springs, we have homes that have a lot of stairs, don't we? How's that going to be dealt with? We talk about modifications that would have to be done, or if they would have to move to a more accessible home, and what that would entail.

Reverse mortgage can be a great funding vehicle. How does that work for somebody like that? Because there was a time, as you know, when reverse mortgages were used as the last-ditch effort. It was when somebody had to tap into the only asset they have, which is the equity in their home, to pay for a caregiving situation. Now, we can go to the line of credit. And if we're in good health, we can use that line of credit to buy one of these life bundled products we talked about.

It is important because it takes less money to support that, and we can use the line of credit to pay for it over a limited period of time. We decide when we build the product and if you should have long-term care. Instead of pulling equity out of your home, you're pulling the funding out of the death benefit. So, you're not disturbing that line, and you're not disturbing the equity position.

What if you never need long-term care, and you pass away, one of the reluctances of the reverse mortgage is, "I wanted to pass my home onto the children." Well, you and I both know, the children want the value of the home; they don't necessarily want the home. So, here's a way to basically have a death benefit, paid in an income tax-free position to the children. They can use it to either pay off the reverse mortgage and stay in the home or take the equity and that death benefit.

Because these have cash values and return a premium, at some point in time, the client can say, "I'm just going to take my money back." With all the options I've talked about, that still leaves the rest of that line of credit with which they can live their life the way they want. They have that line or that equity they pulled off to the sidelines protected by this plan.

Kevin: What do you like best about your business, Tom?

Tom: I like helping people. A lot of times, they look at what I do, and they ask, "Why in the heck would you choose this as a career?" I choose it because it's a very challenging business to be in. I'm so passionate about serving the greater good, about speaking the message of protection. I like to ask, "What's your plan?" That's where I get my satisfaction, from being able to sit down and take the proper time to answer that.

I'm sure it's the same thing for you, when you're sitting down with a mortgage or a reverse mortgage situation. It is rewarding just knowing that you did a job to help somebody get to a better place. In my case, it's getting to a better place under trying circumstances.

Kevin: Is there a particular technique or product you use, about which you wish more people knew?

Tom: I wish there was more knowledge about some of the new types of planning products out there. The only way we can get that information out is by continuing to do my seminars and workshops. I have a free educational video link that I make available to everybody to check out. It's basically three separate videos in which I give you 30-plus minutes of my expertise on how to understand long-term care planning. I discuss how to be the savvy buyer. When you're done with watching my video, you generally know more than others out there.

I am an expert in my field of income protection. When we talk about my frustrations is when people make assumptions that other professionals like property and casualty insurance agent, insurance agent, and financial reps do what I do.

That's one thing that I emphasize all the time. When someone tells me, "My financial rep said that he could do that for me." I have to tell them, "No. They haven't spent 32 years working with this type of product. They don't have the variety of choices, the companies, or the understanding of how to put it all together."

Kevin: Tell me about a recent senior client that you helped, what their situation was, what they wanted to accomplish, and how you helped them.

Tom: I'll go back to the 82-year-old woman that I just helped. She has a very large asset base; she's single, never been married, and has no children. She attended my class, and we sat down together. She said, "I could pretty much, as the phrase goes, 'Self-insure.'"

I always correct people when they say this, because the word, "insure" means "to share risk." So, you're self-funding, you're not self-insuring, because you're paying dollar for dollar. There is no sharing of risk with anybody. That's a substantial difference. But why would anybody that has a substantial portfolio, in that situation, need my help?

After talking through the possibilities, I learned she had her investment portfolio with one of the major banks in town. And they've done very well as far as her investments and her retirement. But, I showed her a way to leverage the existing money she has, where she basically is not even paying for coverage. All she's doing is changing addresses on existing money. By doing this, it allowed repositioning of a sum of money to triple the amount for long-term care benefit. It not only tripled it, but if a long-term care situation comes along, it's paid out to her, income tax-free. Where if the same money stayed in the same position prior to us doing this, everything that came out of that would have a taxable event. So therefore, not only reducing the portfolio that she continues to have, dollar for dollar, but additional tax is added onto it.

The funny thing, when we were in this conversation, she says, "I need to go back and talk to my investment reps." Well they told her, "We don't like long-term care and we really don't deal with it."

This is a large institution with financial representation and this is what I find all the time. Now I'm not saying they're all bad; I've got some financial people that I work with and we work great together. I do the protection; they do the investments and retirements planning serving their clients with a complete financial plan. But there are other ones out there that just don't want to deal with it.

So, I leveraged a certain amount of money by essentially change addresses on it. I gave her the benefit of expanding that threefold, if she should have a long-term care event. And if she doesn't, the asset passes onto her heirs, like it would have if it had stayed where it originally came from.

Kevin: Who's an ideal client for you, Tom?

Tom: The simple answer would be: anybody that wants to protect their income. Life insurance planning really kind of starts when people get married, have children, have things to protect, buy their first home. I cover a very wide demographic. I deal with 20-year olds, up to 80-year olds.

Ideally, I like to deal with someone who is healthy. It makes it a little harder when there are health issues and the client waits until they are much older to act. Like I said, one of the challenges is that people wait too long. They think they're saving money because they are healthy now, while in their 50's. Why should they get this now? They wait.

And then I get those phone calls, "I was in a seminar a year ago, and I'm ready to get that now." Because I've been doing this for so long, I will reply with, "What have you been diagnosed with?"

They are surprised and say, "Oh, how did you know?". Because I've been doing this for a long time and the sad part is I have to say I'm sorry but I can't help them now because they waited too long."

They think they were saving money, which they're not. Insurance product pricing is based on age, gender and health. So, the longer you wait, the more expensive it becomes. And the other thing that people don't realize is, companies are constantly coming out with new products, but they're usually at higher rates, too.

So, my ideal client is healthy. I would say my prime ability to help people is between 40 to 67 years of age. They have something that they feel is worth protecting. And I hope that's their family.

Kevin: What's the first step you'd want these ideal clients to take?

Tom: Usually, they contact me and I send them to the educational link. If they're willing to spend 30 minutes just going through the video, it gives a nice foundation and they can write down questions. When we get together and talk, we can go from there. That 30-minute video gives them a lot of information. It explains the four planning elements: what long-term care is, how it works, what kinds of vehicles are available, what you should consider, and what you should understand.

That 30 minutes watching that video goes a long way. Being able to sit down after the fact, allows me to start really concentrating on what works for their individual situation.

Kevin: How do your ideal clients find you right now?

Tom: Right now, it's pretty much through either attending one of my seminars or workshops because I speak all over Colorado or from word-of-mouth. So right now, it's just me getting in front of people and speaking to the value of "Having a Plan".

Kevin: What's the biggest challenge you're facing right now?

Tom: I guess still dealing with the perception that, "It's never going to happen to me." My biggest challenge is getting past those denials, those stories, and those excuses.

Kevin: What's working for you to attract new business? You said you're doing a lot of seminars? Are you just educating and speaking?

Tom: Pretty much. I made a commitment when going forward in this business, and especially when I came to Colorado Springs. I'm willing to speak, for free, to any group that sees value in this message. I've been blessed with a lot of people responding to that and allowing me to speak. Through those discussions, I've been able to change people's perception of what it means to plan, and we've been able to go along and do some good work. There are some people that are still reluctant. Sometimes it takes multiple times hearing the message before they finally meet with me.

The impact of the guy with his head buried in the sand has been funny. I've had people come up to me off to the side when I speak and say, "That's me." But at least I got them to realize that, to pull their head out of the sand and have a discussion. So sometimes it takes a while to break down that barrier. I've also been very blessed with the last few months doing radio interviews, and it's been nice to get the message out that way too.

Right now, it's just me presenting the message any way I can, and seeing who's listening.

Kevin: What would you say is the best advice you've ever received?

Tom: There are a few, but "Be the change you wish to see in the world" has always resonated with me.

From a philosophical standpoint, I find that serving is always the best thing that promotes success. Selflessness will always beat selfishness. And sometimes we get caught up in things not going well. When I catch myself in these periods where things might not flow the way that I want them too, realize I'm not serving enough so I go out and serve, in any way that I can, in whatever capacity that I can. And lo and behold, positive energy starts flowing back to me.

Kevin: Is there anything else you would like to share?

Tom: There are two books that had a profound impact on my life: *Tribe* by Seth Godin and *The One Thing* by Gary Keller.

In *The One Thing*, you find out what your passion is, and focus on that passion. You block out everything else and focus on that one thing because that's what's going to drive you to your ultimate higher level of success.

Tribe is about taking a leadership role. To take a message that resonates with a group, from a passion standpoint and to continue to speak that message. One of the commitments I made in coming to Colorado Springs was to build a tribe of like-minded people that understand the importance of planning. A group that speaks with one voice: it's not about buying insurance; it's about having a plan. And I have been blessed to find that community, that tribe to help promote the importance, the empowerment of planning.

Kevin: How can people get ahold of you?

Tom: They can call me, they can email me ... my phone number is 800-798-7490. And my email is tom@csim4u.com. They can always go and look at my educational video too, which can be found at: www.incomepro.org/free-advice.

Kevin: Thank you so much.

Tom: Thank you.

CHAPTER 10
Linda Leitz

Linda Leitz is the president of Peace of Mind Financial Planning in Colorado Springs. She's a Certified Financial Planner, is enrolled to practice before the IRS, and has been a financial professional since 1979. In addition to assisting her clients with investments, retirement and college planning, estate and tax planning and more, Linda is also Certified Divorce Financial Analyst and helps people in the midst of a divorce resolve financial issues.

Linda is the author of two books. *The Ultimate Parenting Map to Money Smart Kids* is for parents who want to teach their children about money. *We Need to Talk – Money & Kids After Divorce* helps single moms organize their finances and work with their ex-husbands on financial issues that impact their children.

Linda graduated from Principia College with a degree in Business Administration, has an MBA from Southern Methodist University, and has a PhD in Personal Financial Planning at Kansas State University.

Kevin: I'm with Linda Leitz. She's a financial planner with It's Not Just Money. Thanks for taking time to be interviewed today, Linda.

Linda: You bet.

Kevin: We'll just start off asking some background questions. Where are you from, where'd you grow up?

Linda: I grew up in the Texas panhandle, a little town outside of Amarillo.

Kevin: Dalhart, is that what it is?

Linda: That is one of the places we played in football, but we beat them every time. It's Borger, B-O-R-G-E-R, Bulldogs, "Bite, bite, bite."

Kevin: Football and Texas are synonymous.

Linda: And it's a religion.

Kevin: What was your childhood like? What kind of work did your parents do?

Linda: My dad was self-employed. He had several ventures and the last business he had he co-owned with his brother; it was a regional trucking firm. He sold that when I was in third grade, so my dad was, for all practical purposes, retired in his mid-fifties, and I grew up with both of my parents at home.

Kevin: Awesome, that's cool. How is it that you got into financial planning? What's the path that you got to where you're at?

Linda: When I got out of college, I was a bank examiner for four years and then I was a banker for another nine after that. And at one point, one of my parent's financial advisors, their broker, said, "You know, you understand the financial side of this and you're good with people. You should do this." I started off in a commission environment where I was selling investments. I found that my banking background and my natural love of finding out about people kept me from making a lot of money at that. Somebody would come in and say, "I'm ready to start investing." And I'd say, "Okay great, can I ask you a few other questions? Do you own a home? Do you have emergency savings? Do you have any credit cards?"

That last one was a killer. If they had credit card debt I'd say, "You need to go home and you need to pay those off and then come back and see me." Guess what, when you're selling investments you don't get paid for telling people to do that, so over that time period I transitioned into doing what I do now, which is fee-only financial planning. We look at everything that is a part of a person's or a family's financial life. That may include getting on a budget, reducing their debt, and figuring out what their debt propensities are.

That's another area where I'll draw in other professionals. There's a woman that I work with, that I just adore, out of Atlanta. She's really good at helping people get on a budget and understand their money decisions. Sometimes we'll draw her in to work with a client for a while, but I like working with people. If they make great decisions, or even just good decisions, they'll be fine financially. But if they make some bad ones, it's going to hurt them, so I like to help them keep in that range of those good decisions.

Kevin: What do you enjoy most about what you do?

Linda: It's definitely the interaction with people and the impact on their lives. Certainly, you have to be good at the technical and quantitative side. I can give people all the best solutions in the world and all the math will be right, but, if they're not comfortable with it and if they don't understand why it's good for them and why they want to do it, then they don't do it. So, it's having people make good decisions and feel like they're in control of their financial life that is rewarding to me about the job.

Kevin: One of the big things seniors want is to be able to stay at home as long as possible. How do you advise them with that? How do you help them do that?

Linda: Part of that is buying what some of my colleagues and I call the right-size house. People will say, "When my kids were growing up, a home for a family of five was right-sized. It is way too big for me now, but it's great to stay at home." We will ask them, "What does home mean to you? Does it mean autonomy? Does it mean comfort? Does it mean the neighbors you've always had? If so, how do we structure that so that it's affordable for you and also so that you don't have either too much liability or too much of your financial destiny tied up in an asset that's pretty hard to move quickly?"

Kevin: What type of financial assistance or products do you recommend to your clients?

Linda: Here at the firm, I recommend their investments, and I can implement that for them. Although I can also say, "If you want to go work with a discount broker, I can tell you which investments to buy." I also recommend life insurance, health insurance, long-term care insurance, mortgages, and reverse mortgages. That's where I work with them as well as an outside professional.

Kevin: You've talked about people making good decisions, so what are some of the common mistakes you see clients make as they're coming into or are already in retirement?

Linda: As they're coming into or in retirement, one of the big mistakes is they're either too aggressive or too conservative with their investments. They think that once they're not working and have a regular paycheck coming in that they need to become 100% and outside the stock market. With longevity being what it is, they're going to outlive their money if they do that, unless they have a huge chunk of money put away.

The other one is having too much tied up in their house and they have been very focused on having a mortgage completely paid off. If the mortgage is reasonable, it may be a better deal for them to have a small mortgage and pay that as part of their monthly living expenses than to have a huge amount of their financial capital tied up in liquid assets. I see that, and I also see that sometimes they take Social Security too early.

Actually, one mistake that a lot of people make is they assume that they're going to go from full-time workforce, where their social life is tied into their friends from work. What makes them get up and get out of bed and feel like they're making a difference in the world is tied to work, and they think that sitting in the rocking chair on the porch or playing golf all day is going to replace that. There have actually been some pretty good studies that show over the first six months to two years a lot of people go through some disappointment of, "This is not what I thought this would look like."

Kevin: Is it better maybe to ease into it, in other words, build from a full-time to part-time, to on call maybe?

Linda: Right. It's interesting, especially in a community like this where we have a lot of retired military. When they've had a big military career and served our country and worked for other companies that serve our country, then they jump off that cliff into retirement. They could work 10 or 20 hours a week as a government subcontractor. A lot of those people will say, "If I could do anything I wanted to, I'd work in a fish and tackle shop," or, "I'd work at a soup kitchen," or "I'd be a seamstress for a living," or something.

It matters if they feel like they're making a difference. They don't do that because they think, "Well I'm retired and I don't want to tie up my time." A lot of retirees that are having their best time have all of their time committed. They're either working as volunteers or they're working part-time someplace where they don't need the money but they get out and meet people and interact with people.

Kevin: That's another thing too, isn't it, just the loneliness?

Linda: It's the loneliness and sometimes that exhibits in a financial way, whether it's online shopping or feeling like they have to eat out every day. Sometimes that can bust a budget or cost them money as opposed to just getting out and doing things that don't cost them anything, but they get them out and get them active. Some of those things can actually make them money.

Kevin: I know every situation's unique, but for the most part, is it best for most people to delay Social Security?

Linda: Every situation is unique, but a lot of people take it immediately for the wrong reasons. They take it because they're afraid if they don't take it now, they won't get it at all. They're worried about the soundness of the system, but often they think, "Well, I'm never going to work again so I'm going to take Social Security now." They take it before what Social Security pegs as their full retirement age. Then, if they do go back to work, they lose part of that benefit or it's reduced until they reach full Social Security retirement age because they've gone back to work and they're making more than Social Security, enough to offset some of their Social Security.

They don't realize that between their full retirement age and age 70 they get really big step-ups in what they could make. For a lot of people, yes, the best answer is to, if humanly possible, wait until you're 70. Go ahead and spend down some of your assets or work part-time to cover some expenses, or both, and then at age 70, as long as you live into your mid-80s, for most people they come out way ahead for the rest of their life.

Now, if someone is leaving the workforce because they have a terminal illness and they're eligible for Social Security, that is a different decision, altogether. But, most people take it just because they can, not because they've made an informed decision, but because they know they're eligible and they want to go ahead and get that money. They don't realize that they may be impacting how much they could get for the rest of their lives or even how much they can earn when they start taking it.

Kevin: You must feel sometimes that you are part advisor, part psychologist because there are a lot of the emotions that are underlying these decisions.

Linda: Sure. My most advanced degree, which is a Ph.D. in personal financial planning, is actually in behavioral finance. It's not in number crunching. Because, a good financial planner could put all kinds of numbers in front of somebody, which a lot of times makes their eyes glaze over and makes them lose interest. What really is going to help them is understanding how they interact with money, what's important to them. You mentioned earlier about every situation being different. I can show somebody, mathematically, why it makes sense for them to have a mortgage the rest of their life.

If they're not going to sleep because they're retired and they have a mortgage, then that's not a good decision for them, because they're making more money or their net worth is growing, but they're unhappy, they're stressed, they're concerned about their well-being. There's this whole spectrum of acceptable decisions and part of my job is figuring out where they are comfortable in that spectrum. If they're comfortable in making decisions that mathematically might not come out ahead but that will be fine, then they're are going to sleep better, not because they have more money but because they, "Made a decision I can live with."

Kevin: It's funny you say that. I closed the reverse mortgage for a gal a couple months back and we were eliminating her mortgage payment and freeing up about a thousand a month. She said, "Do you know what this has done for me?" I'm like, "Well, I think so, but why don't you tell me?" She goes, "Well, I can sleep at night now and I don't have to worry about money anymore." I'm like, "Wow, I don't know what that's worth, but that's pretty good."

Linda: Well, to steal someone else's marketing, "it's priceless." You know, when somebody is happy and they have peace of mind around the financial decisions they're making, you can't put a price tag on that.

Kevin: What techniques or products do you have that you wish other clients knew more about?

Linda: One of the techniques that I use is, "Let's put the money aside and let's look at what's important to you." One of the things I'll do with clients is envisioning, "Let's think of your ideal day several years out and what it looks like. What's the best moment of that day? Now let's think why." Because most people don't say, "I'm sitting in my expensive car, in my fabulous house overlooking a fabulous view." They say, "I'm with people I care about. I'm doing things I enjoy. I'm relaxing." If we get around that and say, "Okay, now how do we get to that financial goal?" That, I think is very important.

I think the other thing that I wish knew more about, is you don't need to have expensive, complicated financial products. You need to have something that's reasonably priced that gets you where you want to be. A lot of people want to time the market as investors.

	They want to get a fabulous, well-managed portfolio of investments. When in fact, they would do well if they just kind of kept it simple: if they used index funds, if they got a good asset allocation, and made good decisions about how much they spend and how much they save. I would love to see consumers and advisors rally around keeping it simple. That has some pretty big advantages.
Kevin:	I tell that to people, too. I say, "That's my goal, is to help you understand your options and why it makes sense for you, or not." When I sit with people I say, "There are four decisions you have to make. One, is this the right product to help you get to where you want to go? Two, is this the right time? Three, is Fairway the right company, and am I the right guy to help you?" And you've got to feel comfortable with all that.
Linda:	And a lot of times those last two are almost, in some cases, more important than the first two. They should ask themselves, "Do I feel like the person across the desk from me is doing what's good for me, or are they doing what's going to get them their next check?" If you can't get comfortable with that, you need to leave. You may end up with the same product, but if you get it from somebody that you know had your best interest at heart, that person probably deserves the sale more. You at least know that that person was looking at you, not looking at their bottom line.
Kevin:	Well, the other thing too, is when you're up in years, you can't afford to make any mistakes; you don't have the recovery time.

Linda: You don't have a lot of chances at that point for do-overs.

Kevin: Think about a recent senior client that you helped. What was their situation, what were they hoping to accomplish, how did you help them?

Linda: Most of our relationships are ongoing and so I'm trying to think of a specific situation of what they wanted to accomplish. I'm trying to think of a senior client too.

Kevin: I think the interesting thing about our business is it's fluid, right? People's lives change all the time, and what was an issue today may not be an issue tomorrow.

Linda: When you asked, "What are some of the situations where I've helped seniors?" A lot of the seniors that I meet are in a situation where there isn't a whole lot of room for do-overs. This isn't a specific client situation, there are ones where I help them or, for lack of a better term, reframe their situation and their own thought. "How important is it to you to stay in this home?" They say, "It's very important." "Okay, then let's get the right type of mortgage in place." They respond, "Oh, I don't want a mortgage." "No, but you have one now, so why don't we lower the payment, or why don't we get the payment in a situation where you're better, you know, where it's easier for you to handle."

Kevin: Or get your house to pay you.

Linda: Or get your house to pay you, which you can do with a reverse mortgage. Or a lot of times, this is one of my favorites, let's say it's a widow or a widower, and we're looking at their budget, and they have life insurance that they're paying. "Why do you have that life insurance?" "Well, I just want my family to receive something." Do you think your family's more worried about receiving something, or whether or not they're going to have to take care of you?"

"Oh, well I know they're worried about taking care of me." "Then you don't need to be paying for a life insurance policy that is going to go to them, and oh, by the way, you've built up some cash here, so if we just terminate that policy, let you pay the tax on the cash that's built up, you've got some money." That puts their mind at ease much more than getting $100,000 when you're gone."

Kevin: It's like found money.

Linda: It is found money. I think a lot of times, a senior coming in that I've never worked with before their situation is almost like being in a dark room. They are either trying to find the door or trying to keep from hitting their knees on the coffee table. You flip on the light and go, "Look! You were all the way across the room from the coffee table. That wasn't a danger, and you were right next to the door. All we had to do was show you, here are your resources, and mine."

Kevin: Don't you find that for a lot of people, a lot of this stuff is disjointed? "It really does all connect when we show you how."

Linda: Right, and you asked earlier what I like about my career. Part of it is, "Do I know everything you know about reverse mortgages? Oh, absolutely not, but I'm a really good generalist." When that light switch goes on we say, "Here are the assets, here are the pitfalls we need you to avoid." That's when I can call you, or that long-term care specialist I told you about, and say, "I know this is part of the toolkit that we need to hook you into, so let's you and I get in touch with that person and have them help us figure out the specifics. Either you can tap into the equity in your home or we can make sure that if you have to have in-home care that it can be paid for," whatever it is.

That's not a specific anecdote about a client. Clients that I've had for two years, five years, ten years, twenty years, that's the kind of thing that we've done so that they are sleeping at night and they know what their options are. One of the clients yesterday said, "You can have what you want, but you can't have everything you want."

We all have things we go through and that's the whole triage conversation of, "How important is it for you to stay in your house?" "It's very important for me." "Well then, let's start looking at how that would work. Where are your resources to make that happen?" A lot of times that solution means making that payment either less, making it go away or reversing it so that part of the home equity comes to you every month or when you want it or need it.

Kevin: This is a little off topic, but do you think people just have anxiety about their money in general?

Linda: Yes. The reason that this office is set up without a desk, why we're sitting across from each other, is due to the study that a couple of my professors did at K-State. People have known all along that people have stress around money.

The bottom line is, people are stressed about their money. My philosophy is everybody has access to what they need. They might not have access to everything they want, but they have access to what they need. So, let's calm down and look at what that looks like. Once you know you have what you need, you can take a deep breath and say, "Okay, how do I get there? How do I make this happen?"

Kevin: I can see how your behavioral stuff plays in and so I'm just hearing it as you talk.

Linda: Absolutely. I've worked with a lot of women. I've worked with an awful lot of people going through divorce through the years. But often, my client is a woman who's come to me because I'm a woman. They feel like, "Oh, women are going to take care of women." Well, everybody takes care of everybody. It's not a gender thing, but if I have someone who is scared because they've never been in charge of the family finances and they don't understand the family finances, it's like being in France without knowing a word of French.

There are times when I will literally reach across and take a hand and say, "You're okay. Let's calm down because you do have everything you need. It's not going to look like it did in the past, but it's going to be okay, so let's figure out what that looks like for you." That does more than, "Are you going to keep the house or are you going to take the 401k?" That calms people down, knowing that, "I'm going to be okay. There are people who are going to make sure I'm okay." That makes a lot more difference than, "Are you going to take the mutual fund, or are you going to take the annuity?"

Kevin: Right, and then I think too, hearing you share that people need to be adaptable or flexible to say, "Okay, this is now the new normal. This is now the new reality." It's, "I can never have this again, but I have to accept this."

Linda: Right, and most people, given the choice, will not go through change. There is a quote, and I'm going to get it slightly wrong, "Without organization, all is lost. Without some chaos, there is no progress."

We have to be willing to just say, "This next move is absolutely going to scare me to death, and if I don't make it I am going to settle into something that's just going to, over time, die." A lot of times that whole thing of, "I want to live in my home. Maybe I'll live in a smaller home." You can still tap into the equity of that smaller home if that's what you need, but sometimes it's the getting used to, "What is this going to look like?" Actually, reverse mortgages are a great example.

Kevin: It's not what people think it is.

Linda: It's not what people think it is. It's not all those preconceived notions we had about everything from people's marital status, to their religion, to their politics of it. Those may scare you until you just peak in and look at what's there, because there might be some things that make you go, "Hey, I believe that. I get that. That makes sense to me. That would work for me."

Kevin: Who's an ideal client for you, Linda?

Linda: An ideal client for me is somebody who wants to truly have a conversation and interact about making their financial life part of their real life, for the rest of their life. Someone who doesn't feel like they need me to tell them everything they have to do. I want to say, "I don't have to force you to take advice. Let's have a conversation about what works, what doesn't, that whole range of if we've got terrible decisions over here. Okay, decisions here in the middle and some fabulous decisions here. Let's just talk about which of these good or fabulous decisions would work for you." I want a relationship of mutual respect. I do work with what most people consider ultra-wealthy clients. Most of my clients are normal people who make a good living and can be financially independent at some point in their life if they make some good decisions, but they would be in trouble if they didn't. That's an ideal client for me, somebody I enjoy talking to.

Kevin: What would be the first step you'd want them to take?

Linda: Decide why it is that they want financial advice and let's talk about that. Then generally, we come in for at least one meeting. I usually talk to them for 20 minutes on the phone about why they've called. Then we come in usually for an initial meeting and we talk about what some bigger solutions might be. They can either say, "I only want this one little solution, and I'll do my best on the others," or they can say, "Let's get involved and let's work together for a longer period of time."

Kevin: How do your ideal clients normally find you?

Linda: That's a good question. Some of them find me online, some of them find me through existing clients. Some

	of them meet me in the community or through one of their other trusted advisors. A lot of it, quite frankly, is online.
Kevin:	What's the biggest challenge you're facing right now?
Linda:	I would say the biggest challenge I'm facing right now is working toward having this firm survive me. It's a challenge, but it's not a challenge I'm afraid of because I've already seen the next generation come in and show the potential to step in and care about people the same way I do and help them the same way I do.
Kevin:	Is that encouraging?
Linda:	It's very encouraging. I know how to help people in their 40s, 50s, 60s, and beyond. I think the big challenge for me is how do we help the next generation of clients?
Kevin:	The millennials.
Linda:	Yes, and you know, as I've interviewed for this internship and as I interview for future hires, the big interview question is, "How do we get your generation the services they need and how do we structure those services?"
Kevin:	What I find, working with millennial first-time homebuyers is, generally speaking, they're more financially savvy than their parents.
Linda:	Isn't that interesting?
Kevin:	Yes, which is so encouraging to me. I'm like, "Really? You're asking great questions," and they have Google,

right? Everything is Google and, "I don't want to meet with you, just text me." I'm like, "No, we're going to sit down and meet. I'll text you, but we're going to sit down and go face to face," because you know, it's a big decision. You can just do it over text.

Linda: No. You can do it over Zoom though, because that's one of the things that I would love to have. It's not something that I feel like I need, but I'm open to it and it excites me. I would love to have more long-distance clients, and I love my local clients. I love the people that I get together with, eyeball-to-eyeball, or face to face. But, I also like working with people long distance where we just ratchet up technology and we can still see each other. We could still have a sense of a relationship that's beyond texting.

Kevin: Maybe some overseas clients even.

Linda: Actually, we just had a get-acquainted call with a fellow where we had to do the whole cross-the-globe time zone things. It was a Zoom session, so we saw him in his home library. He saw us here. To me, that's when it really becomes a relationship of, "I found this person and they work for me," not because their office is one I can drive to in a day and still get back home, but because they're doing what I want them to do, our values are the same.

Kevin: You meet with them initially, but then that relationship's already there and you can do that if they don't live nearby. What are you doing online or what are you doing to market yourself to where people are learning about you? Obviously, people are finding you so you're doing something that's working.

Linda: A lot of it is that whole SEO thing, with which I am familiar, but I need someone who really knows what they're doing with it. Sometimes, I hesitate to blow my own horn and say, "Hey, this is what I'm good at, these are the credentials I have, this is what I can offer," but I'm having to get a little outside help.

Kevin: Do you do online reviews or anything like that?

Linda: No, and I'm looking at everything from regular videos posted on the website to blogs. I don't even break a sweat doing that because I like writing and I have a lot of ideas. I'm looking at those and I have to get my head around what really works and get in touch with those people to promote that in the right way. For a long time, I did articles for free in small neighborhood newspapers, and I know what they got out of it. They got free content. I didn't get enough clients to justify the time for me.

Kevin: You used to write for The Gazette.

Linda: Oh, still do. Jane and I share a column.

Kevin: I don't get the paper anymore.

Linda: It's very prestigious to say, "we're the personal finance columnists for The Gazette," but that and three bucks will get you Starbucks. I like The Gazette, we've had some good exposure from that, but again, they get free content, we get exposure. But, does anybody actually come in with a column and say, "I've been reading your columns forever and this is why I want you to be my advisor." That's really marketing, and to what extent do I want to do things that help the public? I'm totally fine saying, "That's a voluntary activity that helps the public."

Kevin: Just a public service?

Linda: Right, but I also want to have clients and continue to grow the firm.

Kevin: What would you say the best advice you've ever received is?

Linda: The best advice I've ever received? Start early, and don't be afraid to fail. I think a lot of times the whole entrepreneurial spirit is people that say, "I have a lot of confidence in this," but a true entrepreneur may have messed up their toe a few times. They may have spent money that they shouldn't have and thought, "Man, I wish I had that back." A colleague of mine said, "We know that 50% of marketing doesn't work. We're just not sure which 50%." We have to figure out the half that does, and I think that's true of everything. It's true of how we structure appointments. It's true of, "I'm going to try this software." You have to buy the software first to find out, "I hate this. I don't want to do this," and you have to buy it to find out, "Man, I wish I'd done this years ago."

Kevin: It's really only a failure if you don't learn, right?

Linda: It really is.

Kevin: That's the key, "What did you learn? You fell down. What did you learn?"

Linda: One of the entrepreneurial programs I'm in says, "There are two types of experiences: success and learning." We learn from our successes too, but if we don't learn from our failures, it's the old adage about history, if we don't learn from our failures we're destined to repeat them.

Kevin: What would you like to share that I haven't asked you?

Linda: Man, these are great questions, Kevin. I guess the one thing that I would share, and it's sort of embedded in this whole conversation, is that everybody can and has the right to feel comfortable with their financial life and don't be afraid to do that. Don't assume you don't have enough money to be comfortable with your finances. Don't assume you're not smart enough. Don't assume that you aren't entitled or can't afford help. If you're willing to take control of your financial life, there are people there who will help you and, if you find people who won't help you, you haven't found the right people.

Kevin: Do you think most people feel behind or, "I'm not where I should be?"

Linda: Yes. I think most people feel behind. I have people who have a very reasonable net worth and income come to me all the time and sheepishly say, "I probably can't afford you, but I just want to explore." I look at them and I go, "Yes, you're exactly the type of person I work with all the time." I think most people feel behind and it is that whole assumption that, "I bet you're worth more, or you make more, or you've accumulated more than I do, or I bet you're better with your money than I am." Shakespeare had it right, comparisons are odious. Who are you competing with? You should be competing with yourself.

Kevin: Absolutely. Tell us your contact info. What's the best way to get ahold of you?

Linda: 719-260-9800, or 1271 Kelly Johnson Boulevard, Suite 240, Colorado Springs, Colorado, 80920.

Kevin: Your website?

Linda: It is www.ItsNotJustMoney.com Actually, even better way, just to find me, www.LindaLietz.com, so that's me individually.

Kevin: All right, thank you.

Linda: Thank you.

CHAPTER 11

Hayden Gregory

Hayden Gregory is the president of Gregory Accounting and Tax Services in Colorado Springs, which he founded in 1997. Hayden has also been a QuickBooks advisor since 1997, and has more than 30 years experience as a business owner, controller, and project manager. Among the services they provide are financial planning and estate planning for individuals; payroll, audits, cash flow management and strategic planning for businesses; and tax planning and preparation for both.

Kevin: Tell me, where did you grow up?

Hayden: I grew up in Denver. At the time, back in 1982, I was up in Greeley with my wife and two little boys. We decided to look for opportunities that were a little stronger than what was offered in a farming community and we saw Colorado Springs. Denver was too big at the time, we thought. Both my wife and I are from Denver; she's from Arvada. So, we decided on Colorado Springs.

Kevin: What was your childhood like? What did your parents do?

Hayden: My dad was a chemical engineer; he worked for Coors at the time. My mom was a stay-at-home mom.

We briefly moved to St. Louis, she got her teaching certification, and became a teacher. That was for three years. Then, we moved to New York for four years and then back to Denver. So, she was a teacher her whole life and my dad was a chemical engineer.

Kevin: Do you work with a lot of seniors in your practice?

Hayden: I would say our practice is growing a lot more in the senior client base, but right now our Baby Boomers are probably 15% of our clientele.

Kevin: When you're meeting with them, what kind of issues come up as they enter these Golden Years, either in retirement or coming up on retirement? What types of things do you find yourself advising them about?

Hayden: The critical discussions usually revolve around retirement. Do they have enough retirement and Social Security? That's a big one, it's not taxed. Do they wait until the age of 70, adding 8% as late as they can wait? Do they have to take it now? We're getting a lot more questions like that.

Kevin: Do they ask about RMD's much?

Hayden: Required Minimum Distributions: they do. Some of them do with their IRA's. Once they hit 70 ½ years old, we do factor in the RMD's and take a look at what-ifs for them. We see if that does trigger any of the Social Security that they have already paid taxes on. They hit a certain level and they have to pay taxes on it again, which is insane, but unfortunately, those are the rules.

Kevin: What do you enjoy most about what you do as a CPA and a tax advisor?

Hayden: I love working with businesses. I love spotting some of the traps that are out there, helping them see those ahead of time, before they fall into them. Every business goes through cycles. When I was a Score mentor for over 12 years, we'd take a look at companies and we would help them navigate through the good, the bad, and the ugly. I have seen some of the battles before and am able to see if a client is coming into some of those battles. I help them navigate through those difficult waters. It's not so much that they're not good at what they do. Sometimes circumstances in which they are involved become a forest so thick with trees they can't even see the tree bark.

We helped a $12-million company in Monument that was making a lot of mistakes. We helped them through those troubled times, and now they're making $7 million, which is a lot less, but the company is much more successful.

Kevin: That must be really rewarding.

Hayden: It's fun. I like to do things like that. I always use the unfortunate statistic that shows eight out of ten new businesses will fail in the first two years. It's a horrible statistic. It's way too high. It should be the other way around; eight out of ten ought to succeed. With the right advice and proper guidance, I think they can do better.

Kevin: How did you get started with tax and accounting?

Hayden: Many years ago, my grandfather said, "Well, whatever you want to do, everybody has books. If you want to be in construction, if you want to be in investments, everybody has books. So, if you study accounting, you can decide at that point what you'd like to go into." I thought that was pretty good advice. I liked math and enjoyed it throughout high school and I said, "Well, I like bookkeeping. This is fun." That's kind of how I started back in 1974.

Kevin: How did you come to start your own firm?

Hayden: In 1997, I had been with a company for over seven years as their CFO. It was a big mechanical contractor here that did $25 million a year. I got to the point where I couldn't grow any further. It was a great company, with great people. It was always family-owned. I decided to jam it into reverse in 1997 and start off on my own. I had one client at the time. It was kind of an interesting decision, but haven't looked back since.

Kevin: The biggest expense seniors have in retirement is housing. What kind of advice do you give them as far as helping them to stay in their home? How can they age in place, how do they modify their home so they do not have to move?

Hayden: Recently, I sat down with two retired schoolteachers and we helped them do a budget, it was as simple as that. We said, "okay, what can or can't you afford on this budget?" We factored in that they both had reached the age of 65, so Medicare was kicking in. We did a budget for them, when they had never done a budget. So, it was kind of fun to sit down and go through that with them and say, "okay, this is the house you can afford, this is the monthly payment you can afford." Can we stay below 30% of their income for any sort of payment and help them decide if the house they were looking at was actually too high-priced? We could see that it was going to get them in trouble.

Again, it's the old adage. Like my grandfather said, "You don't make money when you sell things, you make money when you buy things." So, whether it is a house or an investment, we always to take a look at what price they're paying to see whether or not it fits into the budget from day one. So, it was fun to help them out with that analysis.

Kevin: Is there any other financial assistance you recommend for your clients? You talked about this family that you helped. I guess you don't really offer products because you're really talking about taxes.

Hayden: For our senior citizens, we know the tax side of things. We know whether a Roth or a traditional IRA is a better decision. At that point, we rely on our financial planners. We have a good knowledge of the tax side; we don't really want to get into the financial planning product side. That's when we say, "here's a list of people to go talk to and see what decisions they can help you with, and how risk-tolerant are you." That's the area we like to hand off to that professional side for people.

Kevin: What are some of the common mistakes you see clients making when they're trying to age in place and stay in their homes?

Hayden: One kind of mistake we see is that they'll get to a certain age over 70 and they start talking about trying to invest into a Roth or an IRA. I say, "We just don't have the eighth wonder of the world that is time. You're not 20 years old, putting in $2,000 a year, which, with time, would grow into a nice nest egg." At 72, you're just never going to hit that mark. So, we find better solutions for them, working with their financial planner. They won't have to worry so much about the tax side of things. Let's worry more about the protection side, which is very important for them at that age.

We've been through situations with clients, years ago, involved with Enron. I had a client who had all of her retirement in Enron stocks. She was an Enron employee, with over half a million dollars. She was set for life. She lost it all and has been working the last five, six years at Home Depot as a hand-shaker. That's the kind of thing that we try to watch out for with our senior clients.

Kevin: As you encounter these mistakes, which they make, how do you help them solve these problems? Do you offer education seminars? Is it one-on-one service?

Hayden: It's one-on-one, because each case is so unique. We used to do a lot of educational seminars, more from the QuickBooks and the business point of view. We cover business plans and how important they are. For our seniors, we're seeing more unique problems and questions. They're all different, which is very interesting. We tend to sit down on a one-on-one level. I had another client, years ago, who was in her late 60s at the time. She had a financial planner back in California, who got her into 14 different annuities.

I've never seen anything like it. She had about $700,000 and 14 different annuities. She lost about half of that during the 1980 turn down, but could not get out of any of the annuities at all. It was a terrible financial decision. She actually went back and sued the financial planner and did win some money back.

If we see a situation where all of their investments seem to be an "all the eggs in one basket" scenario, then we get a little nervous, especially with something like that. So, we tried to get her out, to help her as much as we could. We could say, "Here's what the smart advice would be for your long-term planning," and try to get her into more secure, long-term bonds and other securities.

Kevin: What about long-term care insurance? Do you see many people with that?

Hayden: Well that's a great subject. My wife and I have long-term care insurance. It's harder and harder to find right now. With the healthcare law that got passed, we're seeing less competition in long-term care. The rates and premiums are much, much higher than they were when we joined 10 years ago. There is much less competition, and what they're covering is less, which is unfortunate because I think it's a great investment and a great financial planning tool.

Kevin: Do most people you work with have that?

Hayden: No, it's unfortunate they don't. They have these investments, assets, and equity, and they have no idea the storm that's about to hit when they get up in years and need some help.

You look at Medicaid and the very low bar you have to meet to even get it in your senior years, as well as what you have to go through. You sell all your assets and basically get to poverty level. It's very scary.

Kevin: What technique do you use that you wish more clients knew about?

Hayden: Time goes by fast. For any of us who have had kids who are now grown up, it's amazing how fast time goes by. I think it's smarter for 20 and 30 year olds to start planning. Those that do plan are much smarter and much better off. And it doesn't have to take much, $50 to $100 a month just to get in the habit of utilizing 401K plans at your current employer that offers matching. That's free money, 3% to 5% contribution of free money is tremendous. Just having them see that at a younger level definitely helps them in the long-term.

Kevin: It does. Tell me about a recent senior client that you worked with, what their situation was, what they were hoping to accomplish, and how you helped them.

Hayden: I had a couple that hadn't really saved. They just lived paycheck to paycheck every month. She had a seizure that was pretty serious, to the point where she could not work anymore. She is under the age of 62, so she really can't get any medical help at this point. Social Security and disability were working with her to get her qualified for that. She ran up about $270,000 in medical bills. We're looking at going through medical bankruptcy with them because they just didn't have a financial plan. He had quit his job with a small pension. Through his previous employer, he had health coverage and decided to drop it at that age. All they had was their house, with definitely not enough equity to cover the medical bills. So, we're working with them right now trying to get through the medical bankruptcy.

Kevin: Is that a Chapter 7?

Hayden: Yes, Chapter 7, which is liquidation. We do not know what may happen with the house. We'll see what the bankruptcy judge does at that point, if it's going to be exempt or not. They had first and second mortgages on the house already, so there's just no cash involved. They have no cash anywhere to help with their medical bills. It's a hard situation. Unfortunately, we're seeing more and more statistics coming out that the average retiree may have $1,000 of savings or less than $10,000 overall. It's absolutely impossible to survive on that if you have a catastrophe hit.

Kevin: What's an ideal client for you in the senior market?

Hayden: An ideal client for us is one that's done some good planning. Again, we all go through ups and downs, have battles through life, but have done some planning. We are looking at those who have rentals and they say, "What if we sell a rental? Do we keep it as a 1031 tax deferred exchange?" We love tax-deferred exchanges. Those probably have the last of loopholes out there in the tax code. Everybody talks about loopholes and there really aren't that many left. So, we look at seniors and say, "If we hold onto this rental property and pass it onto your beneficiaries, they get a stepped-up basis at the time of death. If they sell it the next week, there are no capital gains." The IRS says, "Yes we've got our hand held out for tax deferred exchange. We're waiting for you to sell and get this big capital gain tax from you." That's been a frequent discussion with quite a few of our seniors, lately.

Kevin: What would be the first step you'd want them to take?

Hayden: Well, let's say someone doesn't have to sell a rental property and they continue to put into a revocable trust. That's the first step I always recommend, because that way they can pull it out and refinance it if they need money out of it. Mortgage money is free, there's no tax on it. If they put it back in the revocable trust, they still maintain control of the asset. At the time they pass away, it then turns into an irrevocable trust on the step-up basis. The kids get it or the beneficiaries get it. The client decides what the trust rules are, and how that passes on to the next generation. So that's a good tax-planning tool that we like to use with our senior citizens. Someone looking at those types of questions is a good client for us.

Kevin: How do these ideal clients find you?

Hayden: Usually, it's word of mouth. This year has been an interesting tax season. We grow 10% to 12% every year because of word of mouth. When a new client walks in and I ask, "Well, how'd you hear about us?" It is usually from another client. But this year, for some reason, Google's been the answer lately. I didn't even know we were on Google. So that's been an interesting growth spurt for us, as far as people finding out about us.

Kevin: What's the biggest challenge you're facing right now with your business?

Hayden: The biggest challenge is having good employees, which we do. It's having people who can help you through the tax season. We're lucky. We've had people for 10, 12 years, stay-at-home CPA's, who help us through tax season. We have QuickBooks people who are very good at what they do. I think the biggest challenge is when people keep asking, "Well what are the tax law changes going to be?"

Kevin: What do you think they are?

Hayden: That's a great question. I've been doing this for over 40 years. I used to get excited about the rumblings back in Washington, D.C., I just don't get excited anymore. They make a lot of noise, rattling their sabers back and forth, and we just say, "Wait until Congress actually passes tax law, then we'll get excited." We go to school every year for two weeks.

Kevin: So, you're not holding your breath?

Hayden: I think some of the proposals are great; I would love the simplification. We haven't seen anything composed like that since 1986 with Reagan. That was a five-year marathon to get any tax reform. It was a big one that happened in 1986. The Tax Payer Relief Act was great. It simplified a lot of things, it got rid of some crazy stuff that the IRS was allowed to do, or not do.

Kevin: Isn't the tax code written to confuse people? There are contradictions in there.

Hayden: Oh, there are. My tax professor way back in the 70s said, "The greatest thing about a tax law is that there are 10 exceptions to every law, so which one is really the tax law?" Which is true, you don't know which one. With all the exceptions, and all the crazy turns for each tax code, it's insane. It's fills up this entire block; it's so big. It's like a space shuttle. It just is so complicated. It doesn't need to be.

Kevin: What are you doing to attract new people?

Hayden: I have belonged to a BNI group for the last 14 years; it's a great group. There are 12 BNI chapters in Colorado Springs. We love BNI. It provides great word of mouth. All over the world, it's the largest networking organization of its kind.

Kevin: That's how we met.

Hayden: I know. I love BNI, I think BNI is a great way to grow our business.

Kevin: Absolutely. That's part of the word of mouth. What's the best advice you've ever received?

Hayden: The best advice is, again, from my grandfather, "Death and taxes: there will always be taxes, so if you go into accounting, no matter the size company it is, they're always going to be faced with taxes."

Kevin: And they don't want to do it. Most people hate taxes. "Here, fix it. Figure it out."

Hayden: And the best advice he always said is, "Plan and be prepared because, you don't want to call somebody on April 14th and say, 'your taxes are done and you owe $20,000.'" There's always that three-second pregnant pause after you say that over the phone, like "I don't have $20,000 to pay my taxes!" So, he's always recommended, and it's the best advice I've ever heard, that "10% of every deposit, no matter what kind of company you are, no matter what size of company, put it into a savings account. Put it in a tin can in the back yard. That 10% of every deposit will always pay your taxes. Then it grows to the point where there's money left over. Now, you have money left for investments and retirement." That's probably the best advice I've ever received.

Kevin: That is good advice.

Hayden: The "10% of every single deposit, no matter what you do or what size you are," always works.

Kevin: What would you like to share that I haven't asked you?

Hayden: Business is tough. In today's market, the number of professionals needed to run a business is overwhelming, but there are good ones out there. To hang a shingle out in the front yard saying, "I'm a contractor with a pick-up and a shovel," you can't do that today. You have to have good, quality professionals to be successful. You don't want to be one of the eight out of ten businesses that don't make it in the first two years. You want to be one of the two out ten that succeed. To do that is hard. Persistence and hard work is everything, but you can do it with the right professionals.

Kevin: How can people get ahold of you? What's the best way for them to find you if they want to sit down with you and learn more about how you can help them?

Hayden: There's a lot of great information on our webpage: Gregoryaccounting.com. Every month, we change out our information. It's a great webpage. That, or call us. We'll sit down for free and take a look at your tax returns and say, "this looks right, this doesn't look right, there's some problems here and not some problems here."

Kevin: And what's the office phone?

Hayden: Phone is 719-884-1290.

Kevin: Great. Thank you so much, Hayden. I really appreciate your time.

Hayden: Thank you.

CHAPTER 12

Tom & Kym Welton

Tom and Kym Welton are regional vice presidents of Primerica, where they work together to help their clients with a long-term financial plan. They assist families with investments including retirement and college planning, and insurance including life, auto, home, and long-term care. Tom and Kym both have a military background. She was Army and he was Navy. They both also held executive positions at U.S. Homeland Security. They're both passionate about helping families become debt free and financially independent, and are advocates for supporting locally owned businesses. They enjoy dining out, and entertaining friends at their home.

Kevin: How did you get started with Primerica and financial planning?

Tom: We were coming towards the end of our time working for the government; we had done that for the first 19 to 20 years of our life. I had reached an executive level with them, but hit the top of the ceiling. If we wanted to pursue a career deeper in the government, we would have had to move to Washington, D.C., and that didn't interest us. That's where we had come from and moved to Colorado Springs. We were looking for a new challenge in life. We had made great friends through youth football. I coached youth football and my wife ran a competitive cheerleading program.

That's where we met a family and developed a friendship with them. He and I became golf buddies and got to know their family through conversations on the golf course, talking about, "Have you ever thought about owning your own business? Have you ever thought about doing something else?" That's when this line of work came up. We started talking about the pros and cons of getting into financial services and owning a financial services business. It appealed to us. We liked the income potential. We liked the ability to help families. We liked the idea of having something we could pass on to our kids and our grandkids. Once we made a decision to give it a go, we gave it 100%. We haven't looked back since.

Kevin: Tell a little bit about that journey and how you got there.

Kym: We started working part-time. We were still with the government and had a pretty significant income to replace. That first year we got our finances in order, made sure we paid off things, got into a position where one of us could quit government service. I was the first to quit. That second year we went full-time. We started making phone calls. We had a lot of goals. We knew to maintain the lifestyle we had already earned that we were going to have to do this thing for real, hit the ground running, hire a lot of people out of the gate, do investments and set people up for success with their finances. The best way to do that is to be an example. If you're going to talk to people about getting themselves ready for retirement, then you have to be the example for that. We got our own finances and retirement in order. When the time was right, we took the regional vice president contract, which was November 2016.

Kevin: What do you wish you knew when you started that you know now?

Tom: We've developed a lot of skills for the financial-services business, which is expected. We've also developed a lot of people skills, which is a big part of this business, not only with your staff but with your clients as well. Learning how to be understanding and communicate better with them. Our people skills have significantly improved. I think our eyes have been opened to the state of our country. I think we didn't understand at the beginning. Your exposure to society is limited upon the friends that you surround yourself with. Most people surround themselves with people that are exactly like them, so you have this idea that the world is a bigger example of the life you live. We've realized that's certainly not the truth. The financial struggle is absolutely significant. It shows no concern for age, gender, or any form of demographic. It's in every neighborhood. That was eye opening for us. Once we started getting out and meeting with families, realizing how much people are struggling and how completely uneducated they are with money.

Kym: The number one thing we learned right out of the gate was that no job is secure. That was enlightening. I was in the government for 22 years in and out of uniform. Tom just shy of 20. Combined that's quite a bit of experience. You hear people say, "You do great in school, you go to college, you get a degree, get a great job, have a good career."

One of the epidemics we see in our country is unpaid student debt. We see a lot people who think they have a secure job in the government that we got furloughed. We lost our jobs. You go from making a quarter of a million to not having a job. We thought even though it was temporary, we didn't know at the time. For three weeks, we were in limbo. What do we do? What's going to happen? I have the mortgage, kids, and life. What do you do?

That's when we started Primerica. Having that government furlough, we said, "We need to control our lives. We need to be entrepreneurs and determine when we work, how we work, what our hourly worth is. Is it worth $25 an hour or is it worth $1,000 an hour? We can control that." You hear people say, "I got this great job with these great benefits." That doesn't exist.

Kevin: What are some of the common mistakes you see people making when they try to age in place and avoid a nursing home?

Tom: Common mistakes we see is that they drastically underestimated what life would cost in the later years. That's probably the most prevalent thing we see. They start making financial decisions about their retirement when they're in their 40s or early 50s and, in their mind, the cost of living freezes at that point in time. They also severely underestimate how long they're going to live. Both of those things are increasing daily. Life is getting more expensive every day and we're living longer every day. The increase in life expectancy is going to pick up pace because of modern medicine and people are becoming more health conscious. You look over the last 30 years at what the average life expectancy has increased; I think that's going to increase dramatically. I think we're getting close to the average life expectancy being in the early to mid-90s.

There was a statistic that said in the last three years of your life the average person spends $152,000 on medical expenses. In the last three years of your life. You think about, if when somebody's going into retirement, automatically you take $150,000 right off the top to cover medical expenses in the last three years. That's not assuming they have medical issues that are going to last for longer than that. It said today, 14% of all their retirement money goes to health care. By the year 2030, if they go into retirement with $2,000,000, $500,000 of it will be eaten up purely by medical expenses. I think people don't prepare for that. They're not aware of it. They don't think about it. It's going to go back to what I said earlier and you're probably going to hear this a lot: There's a complete and utter lack of education when it comes to money.

Kym and I we were invited to teach economics at Pine Creek high school for four weeks. When we saw the curriculum that was being taught, it was shocking. Fortunately, for us, they let us throw the curriculum out the window. They said, "Just let it rip. You teach what you're going to teach." We taught what we teach families. It was mind-blowing. It was so impactful that by the second week the teacher pulled us aside and she said, "Will you come meet with my husband and I?" It showed me that this is the lady that's in charge of teaching our future about money and she was so shocked by realistic money versus school money that she immediately had this sense of urgency that "I need a financial plan. I need to talk to somebody."

Kym: The tragedy of that is because the lack of planning and education, we see a lot of baby boomers that wanted to retire. They hit a certain point where they run out of money into retirement. They're going back to work at Walmart as greeters, Home Depot and Kohls, which thankfully those companies are willing to have a program like that. Who wants to go back to work when they're 68-74? They're not in good health. They're supposed to be living their golden years. Our whole mission is to stop that trend from happening and educate families. Make sure they know what you're saving for today. Are you considering inflation? Are you looking out that far ahead? Inflation is the most number one thing overlooked. You think you need $500,000. You're not on track, you need $1.2 million.

Kevin: I have read that less than 5% of people are going to be prepared for retirement. Is that still the case?

Kym: Absolutely. That's true.

Tom: It's probably getting worse.

Kevin: So, 1% will be comfortable, 4% will be okay and the rest of them will be working later and living with their kids.

Kym: Absolutely.

Tom: In the last 15 years, even more pensions have been cut, benefits have been cut and 401(K) matching has been cut.

Kevin: Inflation's gone up.

Tom: Inflation's gone up. As bad as it was fifteen years ago, it's worse now and it's not getting better. Wages have decreased.

Kym: Raises aren't even keeping up with inflation. You get a 2% increase every other year. It goes up. Inflation goes up 3% to 4%.

Kevin: What do you do to help people avoid these traps or these pitfalls that they're getting ready to step into that they're not aware of?

Tom: The first thing we do is we try to pinpoint what their goals are. I think for a lot of families that's part of the problem–they were never specific in their goals. To say that you want to retire is great, but it's so nebulous that it makes it unachievable until you start getting more specific. What age do you specifically want to retire, or have the option to retire? We always run into families that say, "I want to work the rest of my life." We say, "That's great, but let's still have a contingency plan. At what age would you like the option to not have to work?" They say, "65 years old." We go, "Great. Now, starting at age 65, what type of a lifestyle would you like to live in retirement? Do you see yourself traveling? Do you see yourself as a homebody? Do you want to play golf every day?" We start determining what their lifestyle is because the more specific that we can define their goal, then the easier it's going to be to develop a strategy to achieve that goal. That's where we start. What do we want our life to look like and at what point do we want that to start?

From that period, we move backwards to today and we say, "In order to achieve that goal, here's what we need to do." We talk about a financial independence number. "How much money do you need in order for that to be realistic?" Let's say it's $1.2 million. "Great. You need $1.2 million at age 65 in order to have that lifestyle. Where are we at right now?" Then we start gathering up assets and look at where you're at with your 401(K), IRAs, Roth IRAs. Do you have any other liquid assets? We figure out what the delta is. Where's the delta and what do we have to do to fill that gap?

If that is somewhat unrealistic, then it's our job immediately to start helping to either modify goals or look at more income streams. We don't want to send them down a road where they're going to crash at some point in time. I think for families that don't have financial advisors, that's exactly what happens. They start going down a road where they're not really sure what's going to happen. That's what we want to do. We want to be able to put together that plan where we determine how much money do you need, how close are you there right now, and what do we have to do between now and then to fill that gap? We want to put together a strategy where not only are they going to be able to retire at age 65 and have the lifestyle they want and it will be impossible for them to outlive their money. That's where we start looking at putting together a plan where not only are they going to have a great retirement, but they're going to have a great retirement regardless of how long they live.

Kym: Financial independence in there as well. We'll approach people and say, "Who's your money person? Whom do you talk to about your retirement and your goals and getting set?" They say, "I got somebody." You say, "What's your financial independence number (FIN)?" They look at you like you've got three heads.

They're not on track. That FIN number should be like their Social Security number. That's what they're aiming for. Are they really being set up for retirement? Are they really on track? Most of the time we can overcome that objection by saying, "If we were to sit down with you, we can evaluate where you are and make sure you are on track. It's no cost. It doesn't cost you anything but maybe 30 minutes of your time." We're able to get in that way.

Kevin: Let's talk about a client you recently helped. How did they find you? What prompted them to come in? How were you able to help them?

Tom: We had a client recently who was a referral. It's a client of ours and she is an agent that works with us also. Her mom is in Phoenix, is close to retirement, and her husband's close to retirement. She referred her as getting a second opinion. I talked to this lady and we started talking about all those things. She started providing statements for the assets she had in place and looking at them. Unfortunately, they were not being professionally managed. There was no financial advisor. She was getting closer to retirement, she had done what she thought was best her whole life, was attempting to prepare herself for retirement, but had doubt. Thankfully she had doubt so she said, "Will you take a look at this?"

We did exactly what I had talked about. I said, "You're working now. When do you not want to have to work anymore?" I think it was four or five years from now. She goes, "I'd like to only work maybe five more years." I said, "Great." I took a look at where she's at financially now. Does she still owe on her house? What's her debt situation? What's her cost of living, and do I anticipate that changing in the next five years? For the most part, it's not going to. We really needed to prepare retirement that was going to provide an income stream that matched her current employed income stream. She was not on track to do that. Some of her investments were poorly invested, poorly diversified. All of her eggs were, to a certain extent, in one basket. We started putting together a strategy for her that, for the most part, didn't even require her to invest more money on an active basis. It was a different strategy for the money she already had invested, or money that she was currently actively investing monthly, coming up with a much better strategy to help her achieve her goals. I feel very confident she's going to have a fantastic retirement. She's going to have money that lives longer than she does. I think she sleeps better at night than she was before.

We get a lot of our clients through referrals. We do a fantastic job with a family, put them in a better place financially than they were before they met us. The first thing they want us to do is go sit down with people they care about.

Kevin: Do you find that as a huge concern seniors are outliving their money and like you mentioned before, longevity, and "Have I saved enough," "I don't want to go back to work?"

Tom: The longer people wait to get help, the odds of us being able to help them go down drastically. It's such a difficult situation when I sit with somebody and they go, "Man. You need to talk to my mom. She's working two jobs and struggling financially. I'd love for her to be able to retire." I say, "That's great. How old is she?"

"71." I go, "I'll talk to your mom. I'd be happy to meet with her, but we're probably going to be in a tough spot. There's not a whole lot of time to do anything." Let's get your financial plans in order, because you may have some additional expenses.

Kym: It's such an interesting topic because this industry, by nature, and all the things historically that have happened, it's not a very trusted industry. That's why we're blessed by referrals. There's built in trust. We do a free financial plan right out of the gate. The hard part is getting in front of people because they're guarded. I had a guy once and, "They took everything. I lost everything in 2008 and 2009." They didn't know any better and now they're recovering from that. We're trying to get to people in time. Our goal is to make sure there's time where we can do something.

Tom: I met with a lady down in Cañon City. She's in her early 60s and not working because she's taking care of her mom, who's 80 and disabled. She's living in the grandma's house. The only income they have is Social Security and disability and there's still a mortgage. They're taking that money, paying mortgage, paying utilities, food and medical expenses, which are significant. You have two generations living in the same house, both of which should be in retirement. Neither of them are retired. They're stuck in a situation where they're living off disability. I asked the lady I was meeting with, "Let me ask you a question. What happens if your mom dies tomorrow?" She goes, "I'm dead. I'm done. My hope, everything that I live off of is being paid for from my mother's disability." We see it more and more every day. It's so common.

Kevin: You mentioned before about the study that people roughly spend $152,000 in the last three years. Are you talking about long-term care?

Tom: Long-term care has become an odd product. I don't know if I'd use the word trendy, but it goes through periods of time where it's very popular and periods of time where it's not talked about, purchased, or considered. We're living in an era where it's not talked about, purchased, or considered. If you bring it up, people look at you with utter confusion. Even trying to explain it, it doesn't get a whole lot of traction. Twenty years ago, long-term care was popular. Everybody had long-term care. It is almost a trendy type of product. People don't buy it now.

Kevin: I read a statistic that 7% have it and 70% are going to need some form of it, in home care or something.

Kym: We met a client who said thank goodness, they had that. It was within the last few weeks.

Tom: It'll keep them from hemorrhaging their estate.

Kevin: People have no idea the costs they're going to incur as they age and if they don't have something like that to shift the risk, all they have is their equity or their IRA or their 401(K). We try to talk to people about that and send them to people like you to say, "Go get something."

Kym: What will happen is, it's too late. By the time they start inquiring, the person's in a home or there's some type of assistance.

Tom: They're so old. It's so expensive.

Kym: It's so expensive for them. We do say, "Look, this is something that you're going to need to consider here."

Kevin: It's like life insurance. Nobody wants to think about dying. Nobody wants to think about that stage in their life when they can't take care of themselves.

Tom: If you wait until you think you might die, you'll never afford it. The same is true with long-term care. Long-term care and life terms are very similar in their premiums. You start when you're in your 40s it's not that bad, like life insurance. But you wait until you're 60 then suddenly you go, "Oh wait, I think I might die in the next 20 years. How much of a life insurance?" The company goes, "Guess what? We agree. You probably are going to die. You're going to need to pay some premiums first."

Kym: The Alzheimer's clients are the ones I see the biggest impact on having to go into a home and what they have to pay.

Tom: That's if they're healthy and can take care of themselves for the most part by themselves. Alzheimer's will absolutely destroy a family's finances because Alzheimer's, for the most part, doesn't kill you. They'll end up having to go into a very specialized home with excessive costs and not going to die any time soon. It depletes every penny of their entire life. If they're married, it's devastating.

Kym: Tom's grandmother and mom had Alzheimer's.

Tom: I saw what it almost did to my dad. Thankfully my mom had other medical issues. From a financial perspective, thank God she passed away quickly because my dad already saw the end of the road coming quickly. They made it very clear they were going to take everything. The government sources of money are not going to start until you're at zero.

Kevin: That's an education thing people don't get. Somebody told me one time there's four options. 1. Self-fund, which people think, "I can pay for it." No! 2. You have a policy. 3. You go live with your kids and when I do seminars I talk about this, and everybody groans. I say, "Don't worry. Your kids are groaning too. They don't want you to come live with them. Trust me, they don't." 4. Go on Medicaid. Do the spend down, I think it's $2,000, one car, one wedding ring? You're in poverty. Those are not the best places. It's not Liberty Heights, let's put it that way.

Tom: Those are wealthy people with different income sources that are at those places.

Kevin: They planned and had some guy do it and they listened to his advice. What do you like best about what you do, about your business, besides the time freedom and income potential?

Tom: Being able to help families and really seeing the changes. I've been doing this for 30 years, so I haven't seen a lot of the long-term effects, but even in the short-term. You come back and get with the clients six months later and they're in a completely different financial situation because they've done what you asked them to do. They've made some changes, they've started being better about investing and better at paying down debt and allocating where their money goes. You see them in an incredibly better position. From a life insurance perspective, we've paid out some death claims. When you see a widow who would have been devastated, like a lot of these people we've been talking about, but instead is not going to have any financial hardship because the family put some things in place that were important to them and they started to understand the prioritization of their financial future. They took care of today and then tomorrow and then the day after that. We've seen the benefits of that and it's significant.

There's another guy in our office and he always said growing up, he felt like we were taught you can either help people or you can make a lot of money, but for the most part you can't do both. I feel like we've found the place where you can do both. I think financial services and the right organization can be beneficial from a financial perspective, but we're also in the right place when it comes to helping families and making a difference in our community.

Kym: We come from humble beginnings. We have met with families on the verge of divorce. We have met with couples that were so distraught they were contemplating bad decisions. We get to come in and sit with them to relieve, fix and help them sleep at night.

We have saved a marriage. They were sitting over here this way and not even wanting to talk to each other. A big beautiful home, kids, and she said, "Do you think you can help us?" Tom replied, "I sit with families who can't afford to buy a cup of coffee and I can help them." She started crying and said, "That's me." One of the other things we've learned is you never know what somebody is going through. You can see them driving a nice car, wearing nice clothes, and seeming to have it together. You peel away those layers and they're struggling and suffering because of money.

We've reached into high schools to help educate that generation. Our kids are mostly high schoolers. We've met with clients and older people. We work in the chamber of commerce. We do free seminars. There's nobody that we won't talk to. Our competitors mostly, they want to deal with people who've got money. We'll deal with people who don't have anything. Twenty-five dollars a month they can start to invest. We are impassioned to help everyone. My family wasn't taught. His family wasn't taught. Now we know and we're obligated to go share it.

Kevin: What would you say is the best advice you've ever gotten?

Kym: Get your own finances in order.

Tom: Definitely good advice. We heard a great quote the other day from a guy that struck a chord in me. He said, "Stop basing your decisions on people that won't be in your life in two years." I thought about that and said, "Boy, aren't we all guilty of that as a society?" Everybody makes decisions based on the people that are around them or other people's opinions or their parent's opinions or their coworkers or their friends and their neighbors. Don't do that. Stop allowing people that have such little significance in your life to make such a big impact. That struck a chord. I think it's things that we all struggle with. We all want to seek approval. We all want everybody to like us and be comfortable around us. Unfortunately, comfort sometimes is very temporary and it results in discomfort. I think as a society we're very comfortable with spending money and having fun right now, and not thinking and preparing for the future. When you start doing some of those things, sometimes it can open you up to ridicule and criticism. To be able to step away from that and say, "You know what? I've got to do what's best for my family and I. I have to stop worrying about the people that aren't going to be around in two years."

Another guy told us, "If they're not going to be crying at your funeral, then you shouldn't care what they think about you." If you think about that, you think about your funeral home, the people that would come to your funeral. Then out of those, how many of them would shed a legitimate tear? It is a very small population of your network of people. Those are the only people that you should take to heart and care about what they think and feel about the decisions that you make. All the rest are, for the most part, insignificant.

Kym: We get some pretty good advice. Another thing was, for that first year especially, save everything you make in Primerica. Save it all and be a good example. That was a big deal.

Everybody in our previous employer told us, "Don't do it. Don't go into Primerica. Stay here. It's going to turn around. You're going to be able to retire." One guy even told me, because I didn't retire, I walked away. He said, "You realize you're walking away from $2,000 a month for the rest of your life." I thought, "That's so silly. Two thousand dollars to be here? No, I'm okay. I'll go build something else."

Tom: That's good advice we were given too. Have an emergency fund. We talk about that a lot here. Why do most businesses fail? They don't have capital. It's no different in a business like ours. Ours didn't require a lot of startup capital, but it requires personal capital. We sit down with a lot of families that are small business owners or they're trying to do a startup. That's the first thing I ask them is, "What's your emergency fund? How much liquid reserve do you have?" They reply, "I don't really have much." Do not quit your job. If you can't start your business, while working, then put your business on hold until you've saved up more money because that's what puts everybody out of business. Suddenly they're going to hit a couple of bad months, like every business does, and if there's no money there, they're going to freak out, shut the doors and go get a worse job than the one they left. I see it all the time.

We talked to a good friend of ours who's very successful in business and I asked him, "Why do businesses that, from the outside, appear so successful. Why do they go out of business?" He said, "Usually it's two reasons: money problems or marriage problems." If you can avoid both of those, you're going to have a great, long-lasting successful business. I think the same thing with families. I think it applies to people's personal finances. If you can get your money in order and keep your marriage in order, everything else falls off to the sides. All those big potholes look like old cracks in the ground if you keep those two things solid.

Kevin: What's the biggest challenge you guys are facing right now with your business?

Tom: Realistically, not having enough agents to deal with the population. Supply and demand. The demand is massive. I don't have a big enough supply of people. I only have so many hours in the day. Kym only has so many hours in the day. My agents only have so many hours. There's not enough. I heard a statistic, and I don't know how accurate this is, but I heard 10,000 families move to Colorado Springs per month. A lot of that has to do with five military bases. There are a lot of transitions, a lot of families moving in, a lot of families moving out. I'm thinking to myself, if there are 10,000 new potential clients per month, how many clients could you sit with in a month? If you start doing the math, how many agents would you need to sit with the new ones? That doesn't count the 500,000 or 600,000 that currently live here. The need's never been bigger. More families are living paycheck to paycheck than ever in history.

Kevin: Who's an ideal client for you guys?

Tom: Ideal would be 25 to 60 years old, married, homeowner, and kids. We're not exclusive like that. I'll sit down with an 18-year-old college kid and I'll sit down with an 80-year-old. If you're asking me ideal, the family that I have the greatest potential to tangibly help would be 25 to 60 year olds, married, they have a home, they've got kids. Even if the kids have moved out, they had kids. They need everything we can do. The problem when I get outside that spectrum is it starts to narrow because they don't need everything.

Kym: We get a lot of military, too.

Kevin: What is the first step you want them to take is to get started.

Tom: Sit down with somebody. Sit down with us. The beauty of us versus a lot of the other guys is our financial planning is free. All of it. It's always free.

Kevin: Do you still do the FNA (Financial Needs Assessment)?

Tom: Still do the FNA. Start with the FNA. We've got to figure out where there are leaks in the boat. I don't know how I can help you. I don't know where to help you. Let's get back to basics. Let's get a financial plan put in place. I always tell people, "Our financial plan shows you here's where you are today, here's where you're trying to get to, and what do we have to do? It's going to lay out the steps to get you from where you are to where you want to be. It's going to figure out all those areas where we have to make changes. The sooner we can do it, the better. Yesterday is better than today."

Kym: That bracket he's talking about, there's so much potential. There's money out there that people have, they don't realize. We can help them find it, which is a big thing. They'll say, "I had a 401(K) once. I worked with this company and I think they cashed it out." When we do some digging, we'll find there are old 401(K)'s there. There are old investments there. There's an old something there and we'll find it for them. When you leave a 401(K) with a former company, they don't realize what happens. It's that company's asset, not the individual's asset. It's going to be taken care of for the benefit of the company, not the client. Let's go get that money. It's your money and we'll put it into something for you to help with your financial forecast.

	For us, that's a big win. A lot of people go, "No. I'm okay. I've got this. I've got that." Then we'll find that money and they go, "Shoot. Thank you. I forgot about it" or "I didn't know about it. I didn't even realize they gave me that fund."
Tom:	We've got a good friend in Wyoming that is good with investments. She said that on the average, she finds $5,000 to $50,000 that the client did not know they had. She's finding between $5,000 and $50,000 of assets that they own that they did not even know they had.
	That could be a game changer for the family. Let's say they're 50 years old, over a 35-year career, they had all these jobs. They never kept track of their money. Every one of them, they were putting money in a 401(K) that the company was managing. They had some profit sharing. They had stock options. They had stuff that they never paid attention to. By her going back and help digging through this, she's rounding up massive assets for these families they didn't even know existed.
Kym:	The government pension programs, too. Clients will be working for the state, they'll be teachers or nurses or what have you, and not realize what happens when they don't roll that money out in time into their own account. They can go from here to right down here trying to figure out how they're going to make it. That's why we reach in. What is everything that you have and dig as much as we can to get them as much money as we can for them.
Kevin:	Anything else you want to add that I haven't asked you?

Tom: We try to put together a plan that's going to help achieve all your goals. Just because somebody says they want to retire at 65, that's not the end of their goal. What's the lifestyle? What's the longevity? Do you want to create a legacy? Are you trying to ensure there's an inheritance? These are all factors that play in. You don't want to slide into home plate broke. Most families don't. We've got to prepare for that.

What we try to do for a lot of our clients is incrementally stagger their retirement income with different pots of money. Try to turn them on at different intervals. That helps them to have ultimate longevity and still have some wealth left over, which I think most families would want–something left for their family. By staggering how we set up their retirement strategy helps to do that.

Kevin: Tell us how to get ahold of you guys.

Tom: The best ways to get ahold of us is through email or call our office phone. Our office phone is 719-290-2679 and email is twelton@primerica.com.

CHAPTER 13

Debby Miller

Debby Miller is an Enrolled Agent and president of Phases Accounting & Tax Service. They have been in business since 1987 in Colorado Springs. Phases is the only women and veteran owned accounting firm in Colorado Springs that has 2 offices. One on Palmer Park and Powers, the other on Union and Academy. The Colorado Springs Business Journal named them one of the top Ten Accounting firms in Colorado Springs in 2015, 2016 and 2017.

Debby has been married to Jeff since 1982 and they have no children. She graduated with honors from the University of Louisville and promptly began working to start her own accounting firm. She is a member of the Colorado and National Society of Public Accountants, and is the Vice President of a local chapter of Business Network International.

Kevin: Tell us where did you grow up?

Debby: I grew up in southern California. I was a Valley girl and moved away from California when I was 17. I joined the Army and met the love of my life, Jeff Miller, and I got out of the Army. We've traveled all over the world. We settled in Colorado Springs in 1997.

Kevin: Tell me about your childhood. What did your parents do?

Debby: My parents were both elementary school teachers. Mom taught kindergarten. Dad was a speech therapist in the Ventura County elementary school system. They commuted to work every day and worked throughout my childhood. When I was born, I stayed with a babysitter all day, every day. My mom took her two weeks maternity leave and that was it. We've been latchkey kids our whole life growing up.

Kevin: Same with me.

Debby: I was encouraged to be an independent child. I started my first business when I was seven years old.

Kevin: Awesome.

Debby: I knew I always wanted to be self-employed, somehow.

Kevin: How did you get to this point where you own Phases Accounting and have lots of people working for you? How did you get into accounting and taxes?

Debby: My husband and I got married when we were 18, and so we were just barely out of high school. I decided I wanted to go to college and accounting interested me, but I knew I didn't want to work in any accounting firm. I always wanted to be self-employed, so my goal, from the day I started college was to get a varied background so that I could start my own accounting firm and help small businesses.

With my parents' background in teaching, I've always been very good at explaining things to people in a way that they could understand it. I could do it on an even level with them, as opposed to a lot of CPAs and accountants who put themselves on a pedestal, above everybody. They like to make themselves feel important, and they like to make their clients feel bad and stupid. To me, those are two totally opposite things. I believe that we are a trusted advisor. Our clients should trust us to give them good advice that's unbiased. So, it's just grown and we are now the fifth largest accounting business in town.

Kevin: Congratulations.

Debby: Thank you very much.

Kevin: That's a lot of hard work.

Debby: We're the only accounting firm that I know of in town that's privately owned, and that has multiple offices. We have two offices, and we're woman-owned, by me. It's a corporate model, so there are no partners.

Kevin: Cool.

Debby: I love it. It's my passion. When I get up every morning, I'm excited.

Kevin: That's great that you could get excited about your work. I could never do your job, so I'm glad you like it. What do you like most about what you do? What are some of the highlights, which make you say, "Wow, I got to do this for this person or this business?"

Debby: I really like the business advisory services that we offer. I like to be able to sit down with a business and look at where they've been, talk to them about where they want to go. I like to help them set a strategic plan, which they can follow, and hold them accountable to following that plan and help them move forward to reaching their goals. As part of that, obviously, there's the regular bookkeeping, such as payroll, accounting, and income tax. Those kinds of things are a necessary evil, but as the world progresses into the Internet, those things are tending to go away little by little from an accounting firm. At some point, people won't need us to do their payroll or their bookkeeping. There's QuickBooks online now and a lot of small businesses feel like they can do everything themselves, and only need us for that planning and strategic help.

Kevin: You really position yourself to where you're not just something that can be outsourced or replaced, but as a partner.

Debby: Exactly, and that's what we want to be. That's the only way that we'll survive.

Kevin: Good for you. How did you start Phases? Were you working somewhere else in accounting first or did you just open the doors and say, "Nope. We're launching Phases Accounting?"

Debby: I had set this whole model in place, while I was in college. My senior thesis was on setting up a small business. My original model was a mobile, computerized accounting firm. That was unusual back then because nobody had PCs and smartphones. To be able to be computerized was a big selling point at first. Then, for a firm to be mobile, to come to your office and be able to take care of everything was also another Unique Selling Point, or USP.

Kevin: What year was this?

Debby: That was in 1987.

Kevin: Wonderful.

Debby: I put that model together as my senior thesis and then when we moved to Colorado, I decided I needed to get some industry experience as well. So, I worked in a property management company as their accountant for a while. Then, I worked in a real estate company as their accountant for a while. I was very familiar with and excited about those two industries; they were my market niche. I got experience in those industries. Then I worked in a computer store. I don't know if you remember back when buying computers, you could buy clones and you went and picked your hard drive and you picked your RAM and all that, right?

Kevin: Yes.

Debby: I worked in a local computer store, and I was able to position myself where I was meeting a lot of small businesses. They needed what I could offer them for accounting, and so I sold them their computer system and then worked on their accounting. I did it as a mobile service, after work, and got myself a handful of clients at that point. Eventually, I just couldn't be successful working both full-time and doing my business at night. So, I quit my job, took my boss on as a client, and started Phases.

Kevin: What year was that?

Debby: 1988.

Kevin: So next year will be 30 years for you.

Debby: Yes. It's crazy, right?

Kevin: Yes. Congratulations. It feels like just yesterday, right?

Debby: Some days it does.

Kevin: So, one of the big things we see with the elderly is they want to stay in their homes for as long as they can; they want to age in place. Do you have ways that you help them to do that?

Debby: Well, most of my clients are not seniors, yet. But, we're finding our client base has parents who want to age in place. So, not so many of our actual clients are seniors, but their parents are. But our client base is getting older, too. Most of them are Baby Boomers now, so they're going to be hitting that time pretty soon. We help them develop a plan for tax planning purposes and then we usually refer them to people like you for their financial planning. There are lots of things they're going to want to do to their home to make it senior-friendly. We can refer them to people who can do that work for them and show them the ways that they can deduct those things on their income tax. We counsel our clients on whether or not they should take their parents as a dependent and move them into their home or even whether they should move in with their parents. There are so many different options before going to an old folks' home.

Kevin: Absolutely. That's what people prefer, if they can.

Debby: To stay at home, sure. So, there's things that need to be done to the home that are going to make it accessible and that's a progressive thing. Maybe at first, all they need are grab bars, but anything that you do that makes it ADA compatible is going to be something they can write off on their income tax. We also highly encourage our clients of all ages to look into long-term care insurance and to make sure that they have good health insurance in place. Because, as you know, you're more likely to use your long-term care insurance than you are your life insurance.

Kevin: Yes, I saw a stat the other day from Genworth. Only 7% have long-term care insurance, but 70% are going to need it.

Debby: That's crazy.

Kevin: I know.

Debby: I got it when Jeff and I were 45. We ran the numbers and, if we had waited five years until we were over 50, the prices went so much higher. But, both of my parents have been in facilities. My dad, right now, is in an assisted-living facility here in Colorado Springs. He pays $6,000 a month and he only needs help with toileting. He's not demented or anything like that.

Kevin: It's expensive.

Debby: It gets more expensive with the more help you need.

Kevin: What are some of the common mistakes you see with your clients, as you're advising them about being able to stay in their home for as long as they can? Do you see one same thing, over and over, that they do, or is there something you try to warn them about?

Debby: Well, first thing is, they don't keep any of their receipts. That's a huge thing. That's kind of all across the board because they don't understand that it is something that they might be able to deduct. They listen to people who aren't tax savvy and get advice from them.

Kevin: Like Google.

Debby: Google has all the answers, right?

Kevin: Yes.

Debby: I would say that's probably the biggest mistake that people make. Second, they do silly things to save money that end up costing them money in the end. Cutting corners is not always the right way to do things. It's better to just go ahead and bite the bullet, try to group those things all in one year, so that you're taking the best advantage possible and taking the tax advantages that are available.

Kevin: That's good advice. What do you like best about specifically working with seniors?

Debby: Well, the thing I like best about seniors is, they want to sit and talk a little bit. A lot of my younger millennials, and such, they want to do everything electronically, which is great. I get a lot more work done if it's electronic, but I like to visit with the seniors. I like to know what's going on and find out about their grandkids. They love to talk about their grandkids and I like that. I also like the fact that they trust their advisors and they listen to their advisors. We are a generation of DIY and the Internet, and we think we can figure it all out on our own.

Sometimes it's not until we blow it, we make a mistake or get an audit, which we look for that advisory service. And then, it's sometimes too late to fix it. I also like that my seniors know that I have a large network of professionals that I trust. They call me and ask for names of people that they can trust. I feel with our network of people such as you, that I could send somebody to you and you're not going to take advantage of them. You're going to give them the straight what-for and stop them from getting themselves in trouble.

Kevin: That's the thing; they can't really afford to make mistakes. They don't have a lot of time to recover.

Debby: Right. Exactly.

Kevin: I'm very mindful when I meet with them. If it were my parents, what would I say? I just to try to make sure they're doing the right thing. What are some of the services you offer, which you wish more of your clients knew about?

Debby: Well, I wish they knew more about our advisory services and would use us more as an advisor as opposed to just doing compliance work, like payroll and accounting. I wish they would ask us before they make a big decision so that we could help them not make a mistake. I had a guy the other day; he waited until January to buy his brand-new truck. It was great he got a brand-new truck. But, if he'd have done it three days earlier, he could have taken a $75,000 deduction on his tax return and owed no money.

He said, "Oh, I didn't know." I said, "Well, you didn't ask me." He said, "Well, you should have told me." I said, "Well, I didn't know you were buying a truck. It's out there on my website, about buying a truck, if you'd have just told me." I wish they would call me and ask me and not be afraid. They just don't understand that you can always call your accountant; you can call Phases. You may not be able to call every accountant for free, but you certainly can call me and talk to me before something big is done.

Kevin: That's an expensive lesson.

Debby: It is.

Kevin: Tell me about a recent senior client that you were able to help and the impact you made for them.

Debby: Well, I had clients that came in this year, they are an older couple; they both are widows. They came to me before, when they first fell in love. They're both 90-plus and we were discussing whether or not they should get married. I'm a big fan of marriage. I've been married since I was 18 years old to the same guy because we want to be. We don't have kids, so you know, we're just best friends. My clients and I went through all of the good and bad, tax-wise and Social Security-wise. We discussed whether or not they should be married and made a decision based on the facts, as opposed to the heart. They just thought it was amazing that I took that time to look at all the different options for them.

Kevin: Did they get married?

Debby: They did not get married. It didn't make sense at that point, at that age. I have another set of clients that have not been married and they've been living together for many, many, many years. They're both just getting ready to take Social Security, and we counseled them as well. They decided that they would do better if they did get married. We went ahead because they've paid their house off and all the advantages of not being married that they had in the past are gone now. They're getting married after living together for 25 years, and so I think that kind of stuff is fun.

Kevin: Who's an ideal senior client for you? Tell us about the type of people that you really enjoy helping and that would benefit the most from your services.

Debby: I would say my ideal senior client would be somebody who has a financial plan in place and is open to new ideas. It is someone who isn't afraid of the electronic things that we have in place and is willing to listen to what I have to say and understand why I say it. They would be open-minded enough to know that just because they've always done things a certain way in the past, doesn't mean it's the best way for moving forward, and that I might possibly know something that they don't know.

Kevin: Do you think so?

Debby: It's possible. I may not know everything. I'm not 90, but I have been doing what I do for many, many, many years. I have a lot of clients who do their own taxes with TurboTax. Well, you know your tax situation, but you do one tax return a year. I do 1,100 tax returns a year. Chances are, I know something you don't know, and any senior who's doing their own taxes or going to AARP and getting them done for free is probably missing out on something. At the very least, they're missing out on the advice and the camaraderie that you can have with a partner.

Kevin: Well said. For these seniors, what's the first step you'd want them to take as they're learning about you and your company?

Debby: If they are web-savvy, I would want them to go to our website and take a look at our page for seniors. If they're not web-savvy, then I would like them to make an appointment for a free consultation and meet me. They need to make sure that we connect and bring their tax returns in. Let me take a look at the last three years of taxes and see how they've been doing things. We can talk about what they want to have happen in the future and make a plan to move forward.

Kevin: If you need to refile, you can go back three years?

Debby: We can go back three years.

Kevin: How do your ideal clients find you?

Debby: Most find us by referral, but we have a pretty big Internet presence, so I think if you Google "accounting, Colorado Springs," you'd probably find us in the very top or close to the top. I think for a lot of accounting firms are geared towards business only. So, if a person is looking for an accountant or they want somebody to help them, to be an advisor to them, they need somebody who is willing to work with individuals as well. Not just, "Oh, do you do individual taxes?" but, "How do you work with individuals?" Because a lot of accounting firms, their main focus is business, and individuals is secondary to that. They don't tend to get as much attention during tax season as they should, and they never get attention during the year, because these accounting firms are so focused on the businesses.

Kevin: I understand what you are saying.

Debby: We have a whole section that's geared toward individuals, planning, and moving forward.

Kevin: What's the biggest challenge you're facing right now in your business?

Debby: Uncertainty with regard to the new presidential policies and everyone not knowing what's going to happen. How do we plan? It's halfway through the year already. I think that is a big challenge. Secondary, are people taking their work and trying to do it themselves. Because it's such a DIY world right now and the companies that are selling that software are convincing people, just by advertising, how easy it is to do. They don't come out and say, "you don't need an accountant," but they imply that. The uneducated person might think, "Oh, this is so easy. What do I need advisors for?"

Kevin: That's funny. I've always felt like services like yours more than pay for themselves.

Debby: You see, you're my ideal client. I feel the same way. I mean, I can give most people one suggestion that would cover my fee and, if you take that suggestion, it pays off.

Kevin: Which some people probably are not aware of.

Debby: Yes, and our fees are not so high. We're not charging you $10,000 to do your tax return. Every day, I have people who have done their own taxes and made a mistake or have gone to H&R Block and they didn't do something correctly. Or, we come up with an idea that they never even thought of. Those things, over your lifetime, are going to save you hundreds to thousands of dollars. That covers the cost of our service. There's no way that a good business can achieve long-term, sustainable success without an advisor.

Kevin: You already mentioned word of mouth and Internet. Is there anything else you do to help clients find you, to learn about your business?

Debby: We do a lot of networking; it's mostly word of mouth. It's harder to make a connection with people who found us on the Internet because they tend to be price sensitive. Although, I have some great clients who I found on Craigslist. We put a little ad out there, they contacted us and we met, but it was that face-to-face connection that made it a successful, long-term relationship. You're better off asking somebody you know who they use and then interview them and make sure that there's that personality fit. You can't connect with everybody. I've lost a couple of people this year just because we didn't see eye to eye, or they were always second-guessing me. That's no fun, to be second-guessed.

Kevin: What's the best advice you've ever received?

Debby: Everyone brings you closer to a yes. That's probably the best advice I've ever gotten in business. And to treat everybody like you want to be treated yourself.

Kevin: Yes.

Debby: We learned that in kindergarten, right?

Kevin: Yes, that's a good way to do business.

Why don't you give your contact info so people know how to get hold of you?

Debby: Okay. It's Phases Accounting and Tax, and we are at www.phasesaccounting.com. Our phone number is 719-548-1646, and you can email us at Phases@phasesaccounting.com.

Kevin: Thank you so much, Debby.

Debby: Thanks.

CHAPTER 14

Bill Hall

Bill Hall is a Long-Term Care Specialist. His firm, Bill Hall & Associates, specializes in structuring appropriate & affordable long-term care insurance plans for clients. He also works with financial advisors helping them to understand products, recommending appropriate solutions, assisting with client meetings, and providing educational workshops. Bill represents all long-term care insurance carriers.

Kevin: How do you advise seniors in staying in their homes for as long as they can?

Bill: We meet locally with home care agencies to find out how their business is going and who the trusted carriers are that they've worked with. If somebody has an insurance policy, how well do they do in sending the right people to work with? Do they pay the bills? These home care agencies, Amada and Right At Home, and others, we have some pretty candid conversations, and they're the ones that are actually sending folks out there. Most people don't know that about 65% of all long-term care is actually in the home. A lot of people think, "Well, this long-term care coverage, I'm going to need that maybe down the road, if I have to go to a nursing home." Only about 14% are in nursing homes. The majority is staying in their homes, and that number is growing.

Kevin: So, Bill, what are some of the most common mistakes you see seniors make as they approach or are in retirement?

Bill: Good question. I certainly see denial. When we talk about funding ideas to fund long-term care, if they haven't had any family experience, long-term care coverage is not top of the list. The biggest mistake I see is people don't have a plan in place. They plan everything else: their kids' weddings and college. They plan for vacations, and their homes, and everything that they know is going to happen.

A typical scenario will be:
"Do you think you'll live a long life?"
"Oh, yeah."
"And do you think you may need some care?"
"Yeah, probably." (Because Health and Human Services says about two-thirds of us are going to need some form of extended care.)
"Well then, does it make sense that you have a plan in place?"
"Well... how about those Rockies?"

They just don't want to talk about it. I think the biggest mistake in my world is lack of planning and denial. I hope that's going to change.

Kevin: So, what do you do? How do you get them to a point of decision or get them to consider having a plan?

Bill: I have a series of questions I ask them: "Do you have any family experience with long-term care? Do you know anybody that had a family experience? What was that like? What was the impact of that on the family and to the loved ones?" I ask a series of questions like that.

They'll say, "Well, no, my mom and dad both died from a heart attack. They didn't linger at all." But if you probe enough, you're going to get somebody to start thinking something like, "That's right. I remember my aunt this, or I remember that."

"How was that? What happened there?"

"Now that you bring that up, Bill, that was hard. That was in Ohio, but we kept hearing about it and she lingered." The more you probe and ask questions, the more you get people to emote a little bit, to unveil their feelings. It's not always easy to do. Women are more receptive to the questions than men, frankly. My wife and I have a phrase: husbands in denial. Men are more likely to be in denial because they have alternative strategies.

Kevin: "Won't ever happen to me."

Bill: "Never going to happen to me, no. And if it does, I'll figure it out." It's a series of questioning and probing, while not trying to suggest anything. But, if you ask the right questions, you're going to get a feel for folks. "OK, I do understand. I could have a long life. I may need some care. What impact is that going to have on my sister who is in Los Angeles with three children? Is she going to disrupt her life and come out, you know? My wife is younger than I am. What's that going to do to her? Being the kind of person she is, if I'm at home, she's going to want to be caring for me. I'd rather her care **about** me than care **for** me."

Kevin: Yes, good. Bill, what do you like best about your business?

Bill: The thing that immediately comes to mind is knowing that I'm genuinely making a difference in people's lives and their families' lives by helping them. And I know that everybody says that, but it's genuinely how I feel.

Kevin: I don't think everybody says that.

Bill: I hang around people that feel that same way. That's a secondary part of it that I've noticed. In the corporate world, I was selling widgets. People needed the widgets that I sold. That's fine. But now, my colleagues are fun to be with because the conversations we have are like what we're talking about here.

Kevin: Life-changing.

Bill: Yes, Life-changing. It's about the impact that you have on a family, not "did you meet your sales goal?" My sales goal is: Did I make a difference in somebody's life today or this week?

Kevin: What product, technique, or service do you wish that more senior clients knew about?

Bill: I wish that they knew that there are ways, inexpensively, to transfer the risk that they could incur. If you're talking about three, five, eight years of required care, in someone's home or in a facility community, there are ways to fund it. What I'm learning more and more about is a reverse mortgage to fund that expense. But, there are other ways too.

I ran into somebody the other day who had a big and healthy life insurance policy, a whole life insurance policy with a cash build-up. I said well, "What are you going to do? You told me you don't have any kids in college anymore. You don't have a mortgage. You have no debt. What's it for?" So I suggested, "What if you did this? What if you did an IRS 1035 exchange, took the cash value out of that? There are no tax consequences. You can move the bulk over to fund an insurance policy that reduces the risk."

The light bulb goes on.

Kevin: Awesome.

Bill: It didn't cost them any money. All they did was transfer one life insurance policy.

Kevin: But, they're better protected.

Bill: Yes. I had a gentleman the other day who had money in a CD, making like 2.5%, $100,000. He took his money out of the CD and put it into long-term care, which funded the highly probable expense that he and his wife would have to cover.

Those are the kinds of things that I wish more people knew about and I'm out there trying to educate them.

Kevin: Yes. Sounds like you're doing a great job.

Bill: Thank you.

Kevin: So, tell me about a recent client that you helped, specifically a senior. What was their situation? What were they trying to accomplish, and how did you help them?

Bill: Halfway through your question, a client came to mind. She is a 67-year-old woman who lives by herself here in town. She is a wonderful and kind person that teaches bible studies every week and loves to work in her garden. She was very concerned because her sister lived a long life, but hadn't made plans, so she ended up on Medicaid. She didn't like the facility that her sister had to go to.

I've met with her probably a half dozen times. She said, "Is there something that I can put in place, Bill?" She didn't have a lot of money to protect her from having to go to a Medicaid facility or being dependent upon somebody else. "I've got a daughter who lives out in Ohio, but I'm here in Colorado." So, she's got quite a few big challenges. She's not healthy, and very few insurance companies would insure her.

However, I found one insurance company that would and I coached her through the underwriting. My wife and I collaborated and said, "Here's a copy of the questions they'll be asking." I gave her a copy of all the questions. You know, it's fine to do that, so she wouldn't be totally surprised. She's 67 and living alone. She should understand the kinds of questions that are going to be asked. And she's gotten through the initial part of the underwriting, and now she's going to have to do the cognitive part.

And just this morning, she sent a long note. "Bill, I was thinking maybe I should postpone the cognitive test." They test for the onset of dementia or Alzheimer's and all that.

I said, "You're just fine. This is professionally prepared testing to ascertain whether or not you genuinely have those issues and you do not. I've met with you six times now. You're sharp as a tack." Anyway, she's going to have that test tomorrow.

We're making an impact on her life. Previously, she wasn't able to get coverage, and I think she will now. I actually sent her health situation out to all the insurance companies and most of them came back with "no." There was one that said, "Yeah, go ahead and submit an application."

I sent that confirmation from the underwriter in with the application. And I said, "Remember what your said. And I told you everything up front, so I don't want any surprises. Let's work together to help this lady."

Kevin: You're a real advocate for your clients, aren't you? So, tell us about whom an ideal client is for you.

Bill: The ideal client is someone who walks in and says, "Hey, I know I'm going to live a long life, and I'm going to need care. So, let's get into figuring out how we're going to fund this plan."

Thus, an ideal candidate would be one, obviously, that already kind of recognizes the need and is willing to step up. It's someone that cares about somebody else. The man's tuned into it, not resistant. That's probably the ideal.

Kevin: Is the most resistance usually from men?

Bill: Oh yes. About 70%- 80% are "men are in denial." My wife coined that phrase. I don't know why that is. I think it's maybe the machismo. "I'm the gatherer. I'm the hunter. I know I'm supposed to take care of it." Maybe the need for that is some form of admission of something.

Kevin: We all feel like we're 25 still, don't we?

Bill: Yes, "I'm not going to need that. There'll be a solution."

Kevin: Right. What would be the first step that you'd want these clients to take?

Bill: To sit down with their family and say, "Hey, we're concerned about what could happen, and we don't want you guys to be burdened with caring for us." To have a family conversation and say, "Here's what we're thinking of doing. Like we've done with other risks in our life, we're going to transfer this risk over. We're going to get insurance. We want you to understand and buy into it. We're probably going to put your name down as somebody that has a copy of the policy and all that." I think the more inclusive they are with their family members, the more meaningful it is. It's beyond just getting an insurance policy. It's about making sure that the loved ones, who are impacted by it, understand the steps life takes, that you care about them and this is reason you're doing it.

The funding is clearly a reason, but it's also, "If something happens to mom and me, here's the 1-800 number to call." What's going to happen is somebody's going to call that and they're going to answer. They're going to send somebody out, and

	there is a process in place. "You guys don't have drop everything you're doing and go 'Oh my god' and get the next flight out to Colorado to take care of us." That's kind of what I would say are the ideal steps.
Kevin:	And how do these ideal clients find you?
Bill:	Largely through financial professionals, people that are helping them with Social Security, Medicare and their stock portfolio and converting their portfolio from accumulation to distribution phase. So, mostly, through financial advisors' word of mouth. We get pretty good input from existing clients. We stay in touch with them. We have annual reviews of their policy. Has anything changed? Does it still make sense? It's largely financial advisors and existing clients.
Kevin:	And then, as far as you and your wife, Susan, and Hall and Associates, how do you market your services to make potential clients aware of you?
Bill:	Susan and I give seminars. I also give joint seminars with financial professionals. So, I will frequently be a part of agendas with estate planners, because long-term care coverage is clearly an important part of preserving an estate. We do radio advertising, so we have radio events.
	My wife jokes with me because if I'm within three feet of somebody, I'm asking, "Do you have a plan in place? What is it?" I try not to be obtrusive about it, but more educational. And it comes from the heart. It comes from genuinely caring.

	We have our market. I would say it's largely the seminars, meeting with folks, getting them to understand and asking, "Have they thought about this? Does it make sense for them?"
Kevin:	What would you say is the biggest challenge you're facing right now?
Bill:	Public denial immediately comes to mind. There are plenty of solutions out there. These carriers and insurance companies are coming up with more and more creative solutions that are affordable. But there seems to continue to be the thinking, "It's not going to happen to me." Or maybe it's just a lack of awareness. I'm surprised, honestly, that the government hasn't stepped in more. And I think that there's a tsunami coming, I really do. If we believe that two-thirds are going to need long-term care, that it's expensive, and getting more expensive every year. Less than 10% have any insurance coverage, that doesn't sound good to me. And the government doesn't have any plan in place.
Kevin:	There is something like 10,000 people a day turning 65.
Bill:	Exactly. So, I get passionate about it. Let's make something happen. And I know the insurance companies are talking to the government, but Medicaid's losing funding. I don't know what the long-term care solution is, but I know that there's an issue there.
Kevin:	What's the best advice you've ever received?

Bill: I think this goes back to "listen more and talk less." Generally, listen more. For me, it's to listen to what you're saying without immediately thinking about what I'm going to say as soon as you're done. Genuinely listen. That's helped me evolve into educating and caring to try to solve what that person's telling me. As opposed to, "I wish they would stop talking because I can't wait to tell them about this policy." I think too many people make that mistake. I try to say, "OK, these are the things that are important to you. What can I do–if anything–to address that?"

Kevin: So, to be solutions-oriented.

Bill: Yes, solutions-focused. Listen more and talk less.

Kevin: What would you like to share that I haven't asked you?

Bill: You've asked very probing, insightful questions. It may not be germane to this, but I have to bring in my wife, Susan, due to her healthcare background. I tend to be more analytical. I'm more involved with data and things, and maybe it shows from the conversation here. But, Susan is caring. When we go on our calls together, especially if it's a single woman, it really makes a difference. Here's some guy walking into a single woman's apartment or home, on an evening call. If I have Susan along, she's very disarming. She tends to ask the kind of questions that are more empathetic, more emotional. "How would you feel if? What do you think?"

I tend to say, "Well, do you realize it's $9,000 per month times 12 for eight years?" I start going down that path of being analytical.

Susan says, "You mention, Teresa, your daughter lives out of state and she's got her own children. I think her health is a little marginal. Would that be a challenge if something happened to you, to have Teresa come- " Do you follow what I mean?

I don't give Susan enough credit. The fact that we have been able to help as many people as we have is more because of Susan than it is because of me.

Kevin: Sounds like you're a great team. I'm just curious, what's the average time somebody is on claim? Male and female?

Bill: It's a little longer for a female. The average seems to be about 2 1/2 years, give or take a few months. It's a little longer for a woman, and a little shorter for a man. And more of it takes place at home than at an assisted-living facility, nursing home, or mental center. It's growing a little bit because more people are able to stay at home, and they choose to do that. When you've got oxygen, you've got RN's who are able to come to your home now.

Kevin: And what's the best way for people to find you and learn more about you?

Bill: My website: BillHallAffordableLTC.com. You can go there and see a picture of Susan and myself. It explains the basics of what long-term care is all about and provides easy access to all of our contact information. I picked the website name specifically because a lot of people that we meet with think, "I can't afford that."

Somebody told me it's like $2,000 per month for long-term care insurance. That may be what it costs to stay in home–on the low side. The average policy is $200 to $250 per month for the average person. It's very affordable. All you have to do is massage your income a little bit and you can figure out a way to take that risk off the table for your family. Visit: BillHallAffordableLTC.com

Kevin: Awesome. Thank you so much.

Bill: My pleasure, Kevin.

CHAPTER 15

Ethan Rector

Ethan Rector is an associate attorney at Spencer Fane LLP whose practice focuses on all areas of estate planning, including asset protection planning, charitable planning, tax planning, and special needs planning, and estate administration.

Ethan also represents privately held businesses with corporate governance, tax planning, mergers & acquisitions, financing / securities law compliance, and succession planning, and both individuals and businesses in various forms of real estate transactions.

He lives in Colorado Springs with his wife and three children. As the father of a daughter with autism, Ethan dedicates his time as a member of the Board of Trustees of the Arc of the Pikes Peak Region, a local chapter of a national nonprofit that assists people with intellectual and developmental disabilities.

Kevin: I'm with Ethan Rector, he's an Estate Planning Attorney at Spencer Fane LLP, which has offices in Colorado Springs and Denver. We'll just start off with some background questions. Where did you grow up, Ethan?

Ethan: I was born in the Midwest, but I grew up in the Wine Country in Northern California.

Kevin: Oh, beautiful.

Ethan: Yes, beautiful area to grow up. I grew up where all the adults want to go on vacation.

Kevin: What was your childhood like, what did your parents do?

Ethan: My childhood was good. My parents were very blue collar. My father was a rural carrier for the U.S. Postal Service and my mother was a social worker for the County of Sonoma. I grew up in a townhome with three brothers. My parents didn't have a lot of money, but they made enough to get by and for us to have a very enjoyable childhood. Our vacations mostly consisted of camping, so we did a lot of outdoor stuff. We weren't going on elaborate trips or anything, but we were driving up and down the coast, just having a great time.

Kevin: How did you get to Colorado?

Ethan: It's a long story. I went to school at the University of Southern California in Los Angeles. I went there for broadcast journalism. I wanted to be a television or radio sportscaster. I was a big sports fan growing up. I'm a fan of all the Northern California sports teams and I wanted to be the guy calling the games. I'd still love to be the guy calling the games. That would be a wonderful career to have, but my life took me in a different path.

After I got out of school, I took a job doing sports on the news for an ABC affiliate in Rapid City, South Dakota. I was covering sports that, to be honest, I really never wanted to know about; things like rodeo and lower division college football. But I enjoyed every day on the job, I will tell you that. The issue was that job, or any job in television, at least from my perspective, wasn't going to provide me the life I wanted. I wanted more financial flexibility; I wanted to go to bed at a decent hour; I wanted a weekend off. And I didn't want my advancement dictated by whether a news director liked the way I looked on tape. When you're working as a journalist, it's your life, even if you're able to climb to the larger markets. I just couldn't see myself happy down the road if I stayed in the business.

So about 18 months into the job, I decided to go to law school. I took a communications law course at USC and loved it; I knew then that if journalism didn't work out that would be the way I wanted to go.

I went to Marquette University Law School in Milwaukee, Wisconsin, primarily because they had a sports law program, of all things. I thought I may have the chance to still work in sports and be a lawyer.

It was my third year in law school when I took the required Trusts and Estates course, and I absolutely loved it. When I got out of law school I had the opportunity to get a job out here in Colorado with a small, solo practitioner who wanted to bring me aboard with the hopes that I would eventually take over her practice. Things didn't work out between us, but I spent four years with her, got the opportunity to move to Berenbaum Weinshienk PC and then just recently moved over to Spencer Fane as part of a corporate merger. So I've been practicing in Colorado now for six and a half years.

Kevin: Have you always done estate planning ever since you got out of law school?

Ethan: That's correct. I've expanded my practice since to include other areas of law germane to estate planning. A lot of the clients I've dealt with have business interests, so that naturally took me into areas of corporate law, such as corporate governance and business transactions. I do a lot of asset protection and special needs planning as well. I have a daughter with autism, so helping families who have loved ones with disabilities is near and dear to me. Finally, I do a lot of probate work, because if you're going to help people plan for death, you're going to help their families administer their estates after death.

Kevin: What do you wish you knew when you started that you know now?

Ethan: I guess it's how much the law is truly a business. It's a noble profession. You can have a great mindset about going out and helping people, but you still have to be able to generate clients and make a living, and that's about creating and managing relationships. It's not about how smart you are or how well you did on the bar exam. It's about your ability to connect with other people, find out what they want, and be able to meet, or better yet exceed, their expectations.

Kevin: That's true about lots of things, isn't it?

Ethan: Yes.

Kevin: In your practice, do you work with a lot of seniors?

Ethan: I do. Naturally, estate planning tends to be a bigger and bigger concern for most people as they age. Everyone needs planning, truthfully, when they turn 18 years old, because they are no longer a minor or dependent under the law. But the majority of people don't start thinking about it until they are older. Some implement plans when they get married or when they have kids. But the majority doesn't take it seriously until the kids are out of the house, then they start looking at what they've accumulated in life, and how they can protect it.

Kevin: I think what a lot of people fail to recognize is there's a senior partner, Uncle Sam, that if you don't want him in your business you've got to be proactive about it, right?

Ethan: Sure. Fortunately, at least under the current laws, many people don't have estate tax issues. But it's a political football, and the future of the tax is going to depend on who is in control in Washington. But even if the laws change, we can use tools that may be able to reduce or even eliminate that tax.

There is also some income tax planning that you can try to take advantage of as well, because the more you can hold onto during life, the more that's going to be there to be able to pass on to your loved ones.

Kevin: Exactly. What do you like best about what you do? What are the highlights of your role and your position?

Ethan: It's the relationships, completely. One of the things I love about the law, just like one of the big reasons I wanted to be a journalist, is being able to communicate with people and learn about what their values are, what their desires are, and then being able to put together a plan that addresses them. I love that my clients can trust me to hear what they are saying and

	put them on paper through a plan. It's really about the relationships with the people that I work with.
Kevin:	One of the big things we see with seniors are they want to stay in their home as long as possible.
Ethan:	Who doesn't?
Kevin:	What advice do you have to help them do that?
Ethan:	Well, there are many documents that are part of an estate plan. Through your powers of attorney, you can ensure that the people making decisions for you know that they are supposed to utilize your property as best as possible to allow you to stay in your home as long as possible. If going into a facility is really your "last resort", you can provide instructions in your documents to reflect that.
	Another thing is letting them know the financial tools that are available to allow them to be able to stay in their homes. A lot of it isn't just about the legal plan that you put in place, it's looking at the financial tools that are available and connecting your clients with the right people who work in those areas. You can't work as an estate planner in a silo, you always have to consider the tax expertise of an accountant who may be out there, the financial expertise of an advisor, of a mortgage broker, of a real estate agent, things like that. Having that team in place is really the only way you're going to meet the client's true goals.
Kevin:	Awesome. As far as your work with seniors, what are some of the most common mistakes you see them make as they approach or are in retirement?

Ethan: The biggest mistakes I see them making comes from the lack of knowledge of the law. A lot of times, I have to unwind issues with respect to ownership of property and with respect to beneficiaries on property because the clients are only considering making things easy to pass on. They don't think about the other implications of what they're doing. Are they exposing their own assets to the creditors of others? Are they leaving their assets to somebody who might be receiving government benefits and could end up losing them because a trust wasn't put in place?

Then there's the belief that because you have access to an online tool, you don't need the assistance of an attorney. You only know what you know, so isn't it better to rely on somebody who has training in the area and years of expertise, who can spot issues and make your plan bulletproof?

Kevin: How do you go about helping them understand these things or solve some of these issues for them?

Ethan: It's very important for me to get the clients to lay what they have out on the table. Before I'll even meet with somebody to talk about estate planning, I'll ask them to fill out a questionnaire. In that questionnaire, I'm going to get the basic information for their documents, but I'm also going to find out what type of planning they've done in the past, the financial tools that they may have in place. Is there life insurance covering final expenses? Is there a reverse mortgage on their property? Do they have long-term care insurance in place? I'm going to find out more about their family: Is there a spouse or other loved one receiving SSI or Medicaid? Is there a son or daughter in law who we need to ensure never ends up with your child's inheritance? Are they in a blended family situation where I have to consider the implications if one spouse dies and leaves everything to the other spouse? In the latter case, there's a lot of trust involved. Husbands and wives tend to trust that the other one won't change the plan after the first of them die, but they don't think about the influence that will come from other family members as they get older in life as well.

Kevin: Which tend to be selfish, am I right?

Ethan: Yes. Knowing that information, I'm able to sit down with the clients, have a genuine talk with them about what they hope to accomplish through their estate plan. Hopefully, that plan is not only going to meet their needs legally, but reflect their values as well.

Kevin: That's great. What do you like best about your business?

Ethan: Personally, I like the flexibility. I'm not tied to the office from 9 to 5. I have the flexibility to come and go as needed. I can meet with clients any time I want. There is an expectation that I'm billing enough to be able to justify my position, obviously, but at the same time, I think my clients appreciate that I take my time with my family seriously. I've got three children. Their ages are two to 13, so they all have different needs and desires, and I can meet them more by not being tied down to the office, which is a great thing.

Professionally, I think lawyers get a bad rap, but that's mostly because I think a lot of people, in their exposure to lawyers are thinking of some very specific areas that people work in, whether it's the high-powered litigator that you see on TV that you're sure makes half a million dollars a year, or the guy chasing ambulances that drives you nuts with those commercials.

But, there's so much that lawyers do for people, whether it's fighting at the highest level for constitutional or civil rights, or, at the more personal level, helping someone adopt a child, immigrate to our country, open a business, or put together an estate plan that can leave a lasting legacy. Yes, there is a price to be paid for that, but I've never had a client say that my advice or assistance wasn't worth the money they paid or that they regretted hiring me. I want to exceed every client's expectations, and most other attorneys I know do as well.

Kevin: Sounds very rewarding and satisfying.

Ethan: It is.

Kevin: What product, technique, or service do you offer that you wish more senior clients knew about?

Ethan: I mentioned some of the financial tools that are available out there. I think a lot of people don't realize the options that are available to help them meet their financial needs through the use of the equity in their homes. So many people are convinced that a paid-off home is the ultimate goal, and then they need to give it to their kids outright, even though most of the time their kids are going to get that property, sell it, and do what <u>they</u> want with the proceeds. I've always been of the opinion that if you can use the equity in your home to make your life better, why wouldn't you?

People get emotionally attached to their homes. But if it's not something that you're going to be needing anymore, why not use its value to be able to care for yourself and live the retirement that you've always wanted? Or use it to pay premiums on a long-term care insurance policy? Often times, they're only thinking about the money in their bank accounts, their investment accounts, and their retirement accounts. But there are other things out there that can use to live a better life.

Kevin: Tell us about a recent senior client, what was their situation, what do they hope to accomplish, and how were you able to help them?

Ethan: I'm dealing with a married couple up in the mountains; they're in a blended family situation. One spouse has children and the other doesn't. They want to be able to take care of each other, but they also have unique wishes about where their property goes when the survivor of them dies. In most cases, each spouse will agree that "half of whatever is left is going to go to the people I want, half is going to go to whoever you want." There are potential issues in planning like that in simple will-based planning because if you're leaving everything to your spouse, the survivor can simply change his or her will after the first spouse dies. Trust planning is often more appropriate in these cases.

What made this couple's case so interesting is they jointly decided that each of them would identify separate beneficiaries, and that who received the property would depend on how long one spouse survived the other. I had to run through a variety of different scenarios on how property would pass. If they died together in a common accident, if one died within 30 days of the other, if one died 6 months after the other. There were different variations that we put in place within this plan for these clients. That isn't typical, and it involved a lot of mental gymnastics.

Kevin: It sounds like what you're saying is you can really tailor a plan based on a family's goals or objectives.

Ethan: You can tailor it almost any way you want when it comes down to it. Of course, the law obviously has its limits, but I think clients are often surprised by what exactly attorneys can do for them in their plan documents; the number of choices available to them. It doesn't have to be a blanket document with standard provisions; we can get very specific to meet what their wishes are.

I also have a client couple that is doing trust planning with me. They're in a situation where one of them has a family history of Alzheimer's. We're putting contingencies in place, where, if that person happens to be the surviving spouse, part of the assets in the estate can be protected from having to be spent down for that person's care.

Kevin: Interesting.

Ethan: Yes. There are options in those cases. That's where we're taking into account a long-term care event and what that can mean to somebody.

Kevin: I know there are fees for your services, but ultimately, it sounds to me like you really save people money.

Ethan: I think so. During the client intake process for my law firm, one of the questions asked is what value we will provide to a client if all of their wishes are met. I don't think people realize how much a good estate plan can save them. How much can they get sued for? How much could be spent in a long-term care event? How much money could be lost in a divorce? How much will be paid in taxes? Probate is also an issue. For the clients who have real property in multiple states, especially in the states where probate is extremely expensive, avoiding it can save you tens of thousands of dollars. Here in Colorado, it's not necessarily something that I try to avoid, but it is something to take into account. Avoiding probate is often seen as a goal that everybody should have, but more than 90% of clients don't even know what probate is. We have a very modern probate system in Colorado, especially when compared to other states. It's not necessarily something you should automatically try to avoid. You need to sit down with an attorney and really assess its value based on the client's individual situation.

I find that when I'm dealing with the administration of estates, the biggest issue isn't whether people go through probate or not, it's whether they've done planning ahead of time. Whether it's planning to go through probate or not planning, have they set up things appropriately? Have they coordinated their estate plan with their financial plan or are things all over the place?

I find that the people who don't take the time to implement an estate plan also aren't taking the time to provide a list of their assets to their loved ones. It's not uncommon for a person to hire me knowing little about what a person owns. I encourage people to think of an estate plan as a gift. The best thing you can do for your loved ones is provide a roadmap.

Kevin: Tell us who an ideal client would be for you.

Ethan: Naturally, I love working with clients who have unusual or complex issues that must be considered, whether it involves business succession, tax matters, marital agreements, whatever. There are so many unique tools at our disposal, and we like to have a chance to use them all.

I also enjoy working with clients who have charitable goals. There are a lot of potential options for charitable giving, including charitable trusts. Then there are those clients who want to set up their own charitable entity. You get value out of it, a lot of times, in tax savings, but you're also able to do wonderful things for our community.

Then, as I mentioned earlier, the third thing that's very near and dear to my heart, because of my personal situation, is special needs planning; dealing with families who have loved ones with intellectual and developmental and physical disabilities. I'm a board member of the Arc of the Pikes Peak Region here in Colorado Springs, a wonderful organization that works for these people. Letting them know you can put something in place to protect your loved ones for the rest of their lives; that they don't have to be stuck living in a studio apartment without any money relying solely on what the government gives them.

Kevin: What's the first step you'd want these ideal clients to take?

Ethan: First, don't wait. Most of us don't know when the end is going to come. I understand people are busy, and they may have an initial reluctance to hire an attorney, especially with the cost considerations. But instead of asking how they are going to be able to afford what they want, they really need to ask whether they can afford not to plan, especially when you consider the potential consequences of failing to do it, or trying to go at it alone.

You may have problems you don't even know exist, unfortunately, until you're gone from this world.

Kevin: How do these ideal clients find you now?

Ethan: I want my practice to be based on referrals; in other words, word of mouth. Some of my clients are referred by other clients, but most are referred by professionals I know in other industries; financial advisors, insurance agents, accountants, and bankers that trust me to assist their clients with making sure that their needs are handled. Clients referred by those individuals are the ones who, most of the time, understand the importance of planning before they walk through my door, and they take it seriously. Getting cold called or getting an email out of nowhere, a lot of times those are people just fishing for information. I like clients who understand the value that I'm going to be able to provide.

Kevin: How do you market your services to your potential ideal clients right now to make them aware of you and your practice?

Ethan: A lot of it is marketing myself to people in the professional fields that I mentioned: advisors, agents, and CPAs. I face the facts; people are going to see them, in most cases, long before they ever see an attorney to talk about estate planning. They're thinking about retiring one day, getting the right insurance in place, saving on their taxes long before they think about who is going to be making decisions for them when they can't and who is going to get their stuff when they die. It's the people who handle those things that they'll usually see before they see me.

Their job is to not only do the work for their clients, but also to bring additional value to their practices. One way they can do that is by having trusted attorneys that can meet client's needs no matter the issue, whether it's estate planning, buying or selling a business, a divorce, or, god forbid, a DUI. They have to have affiliations with people who can address these matters.

I also do seminars quite often. Lately, I've been doing a few for local councils of the Knights of Columbus because I'm a third-degree member of the Knights in my local parish and they know that I do estate planning. I've been putting on seminars is a great way to find clients. All you need to do is educate, and the right clients will see the value in what you do.

Kevin: Perfect. What's the biggest challenge that you're facing right now?

Ethan: We're becoming a paperless world, when it comes down to it. The challenge I have is trying to adapt my practice to do the same. It's much easier to work efficiently when you don't have to comb through stacks of documents on your desk. I just wish the law would catch up, at least in the areas that I work in. You can't validly execute most estate planning documents electronically.

I'm a young attorney, so my business remains in a growth phase, as far as trying to create and nurture referral sources. I also got into the practice a little later than many people do, and I didn't have the training that some attorneys get working in larger law firms as an associate, where you get the benefit of working hand-in-hand with experienced partners and learn how to handle a smorgasbord of issues. I've had to learn the law and practice the law at the same time, and I do struggle with that occasionally because there are only so many hours in the day. Sometimes you're forced to spend hours researching issues that you know you can't bill, but you have to do in order to serve your clients.

Kevin: What's the best advice you've ever received?

Ethan: I think my father once told me, and I try to keep this in mind when I'm sitting down with clients, "God gave you two ears and one mouth for a reason. You need to listen twice as much as you're speaking." If you're trying to prove to the clients how smart you are by talking on and on and on about things, you're not really listening to them and what their needs are. And they see right through you. Attorneys who talk too much often know the least. They'll try to fit clients into a box than offer solutions that really meet their needs.

Kevin: Where can our audience go to learn more about you?

Ethan: You can go onto the Spencer Fane website, which is www.spencerfane.com, and I can be found under the Attorneys tab. I also have a LinkedIn page where people in the professional world can see some of the things that I do and people I'm connected with. I'm in the process of developing a Facebook professional page, but that takes a while to get up. It's one of those new ways people are marketing themselves, and we'll see if it works.

Finally, they can call me or email me and I'd be happy to talk to them about the planning process. I can be reached direct at the office at 303-592-8325. You can also call Spencer Fane directly and ask for me. The number there is 719-633-1050. My email is erector@spencerfane.com.

Kevin: Thank you Ethan!

CHAPTER 16

Ralph Siebert

Ralph Siebert is the president of Senior Benefit Resources in Colorado Springs, which assists senior Veterans, their spouses and surviving spouses obtain a little known, little used tax-free benefit, which helps pay for their Aid & Attendance (Home health care or care in a nursing home). They work with veterans and spouses, families, long-term care communities, home-care agencies, medical professionals, administrators and Veteran's service organizations.

Kevin: I'm with Ralph Siebert with Senior Benefits Resources. Tell us a little bit about where you're from. Where did you grow up and what was your childhood like?

Ralph: Well, I was born in Springfield, Missouri. I spent a lot of time in the Army and so my kids were Army brats. I was a prison brat. What that means is, I didn't have a number on my back, nor did my dad, but he worked in federal prisons. We traveled around just like maybe Army families would in the military from federal prison to federal prison. Leavenworth, Kansas, Springfield, Missouri, Alcatraz, and then a little place in Arizona called Florence, where he finished his career and I finished growing up.

Kevin: Is it true that no one's ever successfully escaped from Alcatraz?

Ralph: They chummed the water. Back in those days, they chummed the waters to keep sharks and all that around Alcatraz. Now, I was a little kid then, so I barely remember Alcatraz, but the fact is that, they've never been any proof that anybody made it. There has been rumors, but no proof.

Kevin: Tell us a little bit about your career. How did you get to this point in your business?

Ralph: Well, I spent nine years in the active service in the Army. During Vietnam, I was in Southeast Asia. Rather then ending up doing 20 years, I could do good things for people. So, I ended up going into the insurance business.

I started off with New York Life. I spent about a year with them. I learned a lot about the insurance business there, but I realized that I didn't want to be captive, which means, you only work for one company. Once I got to a point where I understood a little bit about the insurance business, and products, and all that, it didn't make sense to me to try to make people believe that one company was the solution to all situations.

I ended up going out on my own. I spent a lot of time working with organizations that worked specifically with the military. One of those being the Non-Commissioned Officers Association. I rose from being a counselor/agent to vice president of the association with the territory of Texas and Oklahoma. I went around from base to base, and trained people to be counselors and agents, and hired a lot of people out of the military, usually very senior, non-commissioned officers, to come to work in that business. I did that for 17 years.

Kevin: I know a lot of what you even do today helps veterans. Tell us a little bit about that.

Ralph: All that time, I was working with mostly active duty military and we were working to protect families. There were a lot of holes in the military structure, as far as protecting the benefits for family members and insurance programs. NCOA, this is backtracking to the NCOA part. NCOA was to enlisted military people, what AARP is maybe to seniors or retired people today. It was a nonprofit organization that, once you were a member, it sponsors specific programs, one of which, was an insurance plan that was tailored for family to help fill in the holes. They were created by the military system back in those days.

The important thing was, also, it had a special, additional benefits for anybody in the military who might be killed as a result of a hostile action. Instead of a war clause, yeah, you had a war clause, but it was a benefit, but not a takeaway. I was pretty proud of that. We helped a lot of people. I got them help, you know, started in their lives with putting money away and saving some of their pay raises, and things like that.

That kind of got me carried into the night where I said, I needed to branch out. I went back into traditional business and started going into to the asset protection business. Since 2000, really, I've done nothing else but that and doing seminars for veterans. I help people with their safe money. I make sure that they can plan retirements and not worry about the next bad thing that happens out there.

I have countless numbers of clients who, they feedback to me that, for the money that they are working with, with me, they have never had a concern. During the last two market downturns, their money didn't grow, but it didn't fall apart. That means they didn't have to wait for years to get back to where they used to be. That's a good feeling for a lot of people.

Kevin: What do you wish you knew when you started, that you now know?

Ralph: I wish I knew about the programs that I help people with today, when I was much, much younger, because the fact of the matter is, I could have taken more advantage of them. I mean that's all I really do, all of my planning for personal retirement planning and all that is based on these kinds of programs. Well, what do we call the Green Line Indexed Annuity Programs that participate in the upside of the market, but they do not participate in the downside.

Kevin: It's guaranteed money, safe money.

Ralph: Safe money, but, it's that space between risk and safe, because you can be safe in the back of a credit union, but, you don't get any interest anymore. Yes, and the market's been on this fabulous ride for the last eight-plus years, but the fact of the matter is, everybody that's there, knows that will end at some point. Nobody knows when. A lot of people that I'm working with today are saying, "You know, I'm winning right now, I'd like to take some of that off the table, and make it safe and grow it."

I'm in that between space. People that would like it, you reduce their risk, but they want safe money, but they want performance. I've been able to consistently show people three to six percent return on their monies over time, over the long haul of good and bad markets. A lot of people are happy with that.

Kevin: I know a big portion of your clientele are veterans and seniors. At the end of the day, as they're approaching or near retirement, is that what they want, that guaranteed income?

Ralph: The veterans are no different than anybody else. They want to know that they're protected also. My veteran work is also beyond that. I do what I call, my non-profit work. That is about a benefit that has been around, it's very well hidden, it's called Aid and Attendance.

It is a benefit for either a veteran, a spouse, or a widow, who, at some point in their lives as they age, get to that station in their lives where, if they didn't have anybody watching out for them or looking out for them, due to physical or mental impairment, they wouldn't be safe. That's going to require care. The cost of care, long-term care, is horrific. The cost of not having long-term care can be even more horrific.

What I found out about, actually, in research because of my mother becoming in need of help, and she was the widow of my dad, a World War II vet, was that there was the benefits from the VA that were very-well hidden, that almost nobody knew about. I've talked to retired Army generals that didn't know about it. I mean it's just not out there.

I started off by working with assisted living centers all over Colorado. Helped them get their residents to get benefits. I did seminars for the family members of residents in these places and was able to help an awful lot of people. But also, to educate the assisted living centers on how they could then go about, for people that came in later, getting that benefit. They developed systems, so I didn't have to do that anymore.

Kevin: So, you passed the knowledge along.

Ralph: I did. In other words, they could eventually take the ball and run with it, so, I didn't need to go to the assisted living centers anymore. I'd gone beyond that. But then, I calculated also, that most people that need care, veterans or spouses of veterans, or widows of veterans that need care, aren't in assisted living, they aren't in nursing, they are at home. When they're at home, there's nobody there that's going to tell them that there's a benefit from the VA that might help them pay for care that they are getting in their home.

I came up with the idea of doing seminars in libraries for people who don't need help yet. I do those seminars all over the state of Colorado for anybody to come who are veterans, or the spouse of a veteran, a widow of a veteran, or there are veterans in their family, like their parents. Maybe dad served in World War II or he served in Korea. Maybe dad's gone and mom needs some help and they don't know about this. A lot of people that I end up helping get into the VA benefit and to educating them about the VA benefit. Possibly for them down the road if they need help, but, maybe for a parent or an uncle, or somebody they care about, who might need help now, is we can help get that process started.

Kevin: Ralph, that's commendable, but just so our readers know, there's really nothing in it for you, right? I mean, you're really educating veterans because you love and respect those people and appreciate what they've done for our country, but you don't really benefit from that.

Ralph: I don't benefit from getting them into the VA benefit, but some of those people, when they find out I do talk about the other things that I do, you know, where I do the safe money and what have you, and at their own direction, they can talk to me about that if they want to. There is no quid pro quo for me. In other words, most of the veterans that I end up helping aren't even in the position to talk to me about money, because they don't have it.

Kevin: That's so generous, Ralph. That's amazing. How did you come about focusing your business on helping seniors?

Ralph: Well, I started to become one. When I went into the insurance business I was 31-years-old. Most of the people I was talking to were mid-Level NCOs who were in their late 20s and their early 30s. As time went by, and as I got older, I kept advancing the people I wanted to talk to, as people more like me. I got to a point where I started doing my own retirement planning. I wanted to be safe, so I started getting into the idea of safe money.

I spent a lot of time studying it and deciding how I would approach it. Then I said, from this point forward, I'm going to talk to people who are at least in a point in their lives, where they either see that time coming, that sooner than later, to be retired, or they are retired, or they're right in the process of retiring. Because, I can really help an awful lot of those people secure that retirement. I think it just evolved, that as I got older, I wanted to talk to people that were older.

Kevin: What are some of the main concerns you hear as you work with the senior clients?

Ralph: The main concerns that I think they mostly would have before they even find out what I can do is, do I have enough money to live the rest of my life? I don't want to run out of money before I'm gone. In other words, I want to be able to have an income that lasts as long as I do.

That's my forte. That's the thing that I can do, is make sure, that, for whatever they want to work with me, that they can know that whatever income they can create with that money, it will never go away, so long as they're around to cash those checks. Even if the account balances on those accounts go to zero, the companies will continue to write them checks. That is the beauty of it. With that safety, with that security, makes my clients feel good and it definitely makes me feel good, because I feel like I'm really, really helping people.

Kevin: Maybe you just answered my next question, but "What are the highlights of your role of your position?"

Ralph: Well, you're probably right. The highlights of my role is, the fact is, that in all the time I've been doing this, and we're now talking about 17 years concentrating on this, I've never had a client come back to me and say, "Gee, I wish I hadn't done that, because having my money safe does not concern me. Knowing that I can create an income. Knowing that it's going to be there, outweighs the idea that I might have made more money if the markets were always good."

Kevin: Really, what you're doing, if I can simplify it in layman's terms, so to speak is, you're offering peace of mind, less anxiety, and diminished fear.

Ralph: One of the companies that I use, the founder of the company said that, "Here's what we do in our company. We sell sleep insurance." I said, "If you're older and you're in retirement, or you're close to retirement, and you see a two or three year turn in the market that goes the wrong way, that can cause you to lose sleep. It can cause you stress. It can cause you a lot of anxiety. The fact of the matter is, there is no anxiety with these programs."

Now, it can come to pass, that if you're in a long upturn like we are right now, we're eight years plus with what is characterized as a bull market, is that people would say, "Well, you know, I might have made more money, had I not moved." But, I'll tell you when they're going to love me, is when it flips. Because the next time the market goes the wrong way, nothing bad will happen to them with the money that they have with me.

Kevin: One of the things we see as we work with seniors is, they want to stay at home as long as they can. They want to age in place. How do you advise your clients so that they can age in place?

Ralph: Well, that would be the goal anyway. I mean, the goal would be to be able to live out their lives and hopefully maintain their lifestyle. The other thing that

I'm always concerned with is, that the odds are, once you're retired and you get down the road, one of us is going to bury the other. Because of that, we also got to look at, how will that affect the one that is left, with their survivability.

You got to look at not just that retirement income and then it's always there. The other things that can complicate that, i.e., if one of them is the principle bread winner and there was no provisions in the retirement monies that they're getting from maybe their pensions or what have you, to pass it to the spouse. Then, how do we make sure that that spouse is financially okay? Back in the day when I was doing the young military and stuff, a lot of times, we had soldiers or early retirees that died and we had widows that, they thought they were taken care of. They found out, and sometimes I was somebody that had to tell them that, they were in a bad spot. That stuck with me.

That is also very, very important to me, is that, the people that I work with, not only are looking to protect the retirement for them as a couple, but they're trying to protect one for the other, should, as is likely, that one predecease the other. We want to make sure that person is okay.

Kevin: Absolutely. As you work with the seniors in particular, what are some of the common mistakes you see them make as they approach or are in retirement?

Ralph: I'm not a person who tells anybody they're making a mistake. I don't even tell people they should work with me. I think they typically know what the mistakes are. Now, I mean there are dangers. I mean, if you don't legally protect yourself and there are problems that can happen, that's why we have an attorney that works with us. She has worked with me for the last seven-plus years. She helps them protect themselves against the legal pitfalls that can befall you. We cover the legal.

The second one is the long-term care issue. Of course, for veterans, I'm helping them, should it come to pass, with the money that the VA might be able to help them with. There are also programs that I can help them with that can offset that catastrophic cost of care. Some of them are very innovative. They're not the traditional long-term care plans that are very expensive.

Kevin: Let me ask you a quick question about long-term care. Is it safe to say that, somebody could of worked their whole life, they've got their nest egg, their home equity, whatever. They're set for retirement. But, a chunk of that or maybe all of that could be spent on taking care of one or the other in their senior years with long-term care expenses? If they don't have the insurance?

Ralph: If they don't have the insurance, they don't know about the VA benefit, if they're veterans, it could or couldn't come into play. I couldn't tell you how many times I've had people that has happened to. They've run out of money. Once that happens, there's nothing you can do. The only option at that point in time is, they do what's called 'the spend down.' They spend down to where the government says they'll help you with care. That comes with its own set of obligations to the government also. Medicaid is not going to continue to be solvent. Even that last resort, I can foresee a day when that may not be there.

Kevin: You were talking about how you help seniors. Long-term care, and legal protection.

Ralph: Sure. The long-term care issue is something that we look at. Like I said, there's a lot of innovative ways to deal with it, where you don't feel like you're spending thousands every year and it's 50/50 maybe, that you will never use that benefit. Just like your car, your home, or whatever. You don't buy those insurance protections because you want to use those benefits. You use them because it can happen. The odds are better than 50/50 that, if you live long enough, you're going to need some care in your life.

Then the third, the last issue, is the retirement issue. Let's forget about taking care of long-term care. You got your legal ducks in a row. You still have the issue of, "Can I retire, from now on?" If a bad thing happens out there, to the economy or whatever, can I still retire? That's where I work. That's my space. That's the place we're with people that work with me to ensure that maybe some of their money is setup to get through the bad times and continue to function for them, so that they have the fallback.

I need to reiterate, I've never to this day, ever told anybody they should move money from any place to any place. When they come to talk to me, they want to talk about those things. What I show them is, based on what they feed to me is, I show them how a program might work and then they could decide if they feel like that's a good idea or not. I'm proud of the way I work, because, I do not tell people that they should or shouldn't do anything.

Kevin: What do you like best about your business?

Ralph: The feeling I get when I have people come back to me and say, "Man, I'll tell you Ralph, it was a really good thing that I did." I go back to the life insurance business. I've delivered death checks. I've delivered checks to widows or widowers. That doesn't replace that loved one that they lost, but it can help them be able to mourn that loss. If you're all of a sudden in this catastrophic financial situation, you're not mourning, anything other than how am I going to live. I've seen it all too often. I know, I know how to help people, not be there.

When I have done that and I know that because of what I did with them, they're not going to have that situation to be in. Then, by golly, yeah, that is something that keeps me, at this point in my life, wanting to get up and go to work, because it's not work.

Kevin: Bad days are coming for all of us at some point. What you can do is, help minimize some of the impact that those days have.

Ralph: That's the goal. That's what I feel like I'm able to bring to the table. As long as I feel like I can contribute and God and my wife say it's okay, I will probably keep doing this.

Kevin: What product or technique or service do you offer that you wish more of your senior clients knew about?

Ralph: Everything I do.

Kevin: I've been to your seminar and I met with you personally myself and, I can say, what you're saying is absolutely true. That you truly have products that can really, significantly help people if they're willing to investigate, take the time, and think about how it might fit for their situation.

Ralph: That's exactly what I want them to do. I want them to look at what's possible and then make an informed decision, if that's a fit for them or not. I can feel good about what I did with the people, rather they become my clients or not, if I know that I gave them a chance to make an informed decision. At that point, it's completely up to them. I'm always good with that.

As a matter of fact, one of the things that shocks a lot of people when they come to see me is, if it turns out they've already done these things, and they've dealt with the legal, they've dealt with the long-term care, and they've dealt with the what if, you know, as far a being able to retire and always be able to be retired and never run out of money, I'm the guy that might sit there and look at them and say, "You know what, don't let anybody talk you out of doing what you're doing, because, you're okay. And, you're going to be okay." They look at me like, "Well, wait a minute, there's nothing you want me to do with you?" I said, "No. Why should there be? You've done it, so, feel good about it." You know what? They walk out of there feeling real good. They got that second opinion and it wasn't the second opinion they were expecting.

Kevin: Tell us about a recent senior client you worked with. Tell us about their situation, what they were hoping to accomplish and how you helped them.

Ralph: Rather than kind of just characterizing this for a specific client or something, maybe, what I would talk about is that, the people that I feel the best about, were the ones that came into my office, really worried about, are they going to be okay. Once we got together and we worked together, and we had done what we were going to do, they had made the decision to use the things that I could bring to the table. That they could look at me and say, "Okay, now I feel like I'm okay. Now, I feel like I can retire. Now I feel like that I know that I will never run out of money and I'm not worried about the next bad thing."

Kevin: You helped them close some of the gaps.

Ralph: That's exactly right. Not everybody comes to see me that has a situation that I can save them from or help them with. But, the fact of the matter is, is that, a lot of people I can. Sometimes, it's nothing more than advice. It's not something I can do, it's something that I can tell and I can draw on the experience I've had with the thousands and thousands of people that have come to see me. Where I've been able to maybe get them to another source that might be able to help them. It's not what I do, but I might refer them to it. The idea is, is when somebody comes to see me, becoming a client or not, I want them to leave feeling like they were glad they came. That's good enough.

Kevin: Tell us, who's an ideal client for you, Ralph?

Ralph: People who come to me that are concerned about, are they going to be able to retire. It's really those people. I mean, I get people to come in and they know they're okay. They have four pensions. As long as the government checks don't bounce, they're fine. That's not my ideal client.

My ideal client is the person that isn't sure. The person that maybe did put some money away in their life, but they're not sure it's enough. They're not sure it's going to get them where they need to be. We go through it and we talk about it. If they then feel like there are some gaps there, than I say, "Well then, you want to look at some possible solutions?" Typically, they'll say, "Yeah. Let's do that." We'll either come to over time or come to a position where they'll either say, it works for me or it doesn't. The ideal person is somebody that wasn't sure, was nervous, and, as long as they didn't make a terrible mistake going forward, they still should have been okay. That's where I work.

Kevin: What's the first step you'd want these ideal clients to take?

Ralph: See me. There's no charge for me when I'm helping a veteran. There never will be and there's no charge from me to have people come talk to me. The fact of the matter is, if I don't do something with what I do, the green line programs that I help them with, or the long-term care, innovative care programs that I help them with, then, okay, maybe I did do something to help get them to a source or something.

But, the idea is, is that I don't feel like they should pay for my time, and besides that, with the programs I work with, they won't pay me even if they work with me, because the companies I work with will pay me out of their general operating funds. I will never, ever have, never will, charge a fee for my work.

Kevin: Wow. How do you currently market your services to make potential clients aware of you and what you do?

Ralph: Mostly, I do the informational seminars. I do traditional dinner seminars at some of the nicer restaurants around Colorado. Then, I do the veteran seminars in libraries. And then, I get clients. Clients bring me clients. We do events with clients. I have a lot of fun with clients.

Just last night, I had an event where I had actually more clients there than I had people who had never met me before. It was a ball. It was a blast, because I get to play with these guys. I was having a lot of fun. My appointment setter, who signs everybody in and all that said, "Boy, Ralph, you were going off crazy last night." I said, "Yeah, because I can mess with people I know." That fed to the other people that didn't know me and as a result, some of those people that didn't know me, are going to want to know me. Clients are my best possible source, because they're reaffirming that they made a good decision by leading other people to me.

Kevin: What's the biggest challenge you're facing right now?

Ralph: Being in my 60s and deciding how much I want to work every week and all that. The great thing about my job is, I get to make that call. I feel like I've never been better at doing what I do than I am now. I wish I was where I am today 20 years ago, because obviously, you know, everybody would say, "I'd like to be able to go back and say I wish I knew then what I know now." The fact of the matter is, I continue to try to get better at what I do. I'm still going to training. I was in training a week ago in Las Vegas. I continue to try to get better, because, if I'm better, that means I better serve the people that I work with.

Kevin: What's the best advice you've ever received?

Ralph: Go to work. See, I'll put it this way, you remember, what was the movie, the martial art movie, wax on wax off?

Kevin: Karate Kid?

Ralph: Yeah. The Karate Kid. Remember, essentially, he was saying you learn because you keep doing, you keep doing, you keep doing. When I first came into this business in my 30s, I asked a guy in the same business this question, "What is the most important thing you can learn in this business or do in this business to be successful?" He said three things. "See the people. See the people. See the people." Guess what? That's still true.

Kevin: Where could our audience go to learn more about you?

Ralph: Well, you can contact me at Senior Benefit Resources and just give us a call and tell us what you want to find out about. 719-597-8387.

CHAPTER 17

Kelsie Heermans

Kelsie was born and raised in Minnesota. After high school she moved to Denver to complete her Bachelor's in Health Care Management with an emphasis in Gerontology. Serving seniors has always been her passion and she feels fortunate to be working with so many great professionals. Kelsie is a certified as an Assisted Living Administrator in Colorado, and has done training in Alzheimer's and dementia as well.

Kevin: I'm with Kelsie Heermans. She's the executive director of Senior Resource Council. Thank you for taking the time Kelsie.

Kelsie: Of course.

Kevin: Tell us a little about yourself. Where did you grow up, where are you from?

Kelsie: I grew up in Hutchinson, Minnesota. Small town. I was there until I graduated high school and came out to Denver.

Kevin: You don't miss the winters in Minnesota I guess.

Kelsie: No, absolutely not. I do miss the summers though. The lakes are one thing I do miss.

Kevin: We don't have as much water here.

Kelsie: No. Not even close.

Kevin: Is it true the state bird in Minnesota's a mosquito?

Kelsie: Yes. That is true. Absolutely.

Kevin: Mosquitoes like me a lot. What was your childhood like? What did you do growing up? What did your parents do?

Kelsie: Great childhood. Small town, one of those towns where you feel like everybody knows everybody. One high school. My dad was a lawyer so he had his own practice there and my mom was for the most part a stay at home mom. She took care of the kids and made sure we were all fed and happy. We lived on a cul-de-sac and every single one of our neighbors were friends of ours and so just a fun upbringing, close knit neighborhood.

Kevin: All American neighborhood, all American childhood.

Kelsie: Exactly. Pretty much.

Kevin: Tell us how you got to this place where you're the executive director of the Senior Resource Council.

Kelsie: I'll give you the shortened version. When I was 16 I started working at the only assisted living facility in our small town. I worked in the kitchen so I prepared the meals for the residents that lived there. I served them, cleaned up and went home. That's when my interest sparked to get into the senior world. My grandmother had Alzheimer's disease. Watching that whole process, and when she passed away I really realized that I wanted to make it my goal to educate other people about aging, about Alzheimer's and dementia. I suppose I was fearful of it, being at that age and not having any information about the disease. That's how I got started into senior care. Went to college in Denver and got my healthcare management and gerontology degree. I went to Metro. At the time it was Metro College. Now it's Metro University.

Kevin: You said you started in this position in December. You're still meeting people and there are a lot of them. How big is your organization? How many members do you have?

Kelsie: At this point, we are almost up to 150 members. Lots of different organizations and companies involved. Like I said, I have been in senior care pretty much since I was a teenager. The industry is not new to me. This particular position is because I've always worked at facilities and communities whether it's nursing home, assisted living. This is fun to be on the other side and really support those professionals that are still working really in the depths of senior care.

Kevin: Yeah. What do you wish you knew when you started that you know now?

Kelsie: Well, I think that it probably would've been good to know how to navigate getting so close to all of the residents. I look back, I can't even count how many seniors I became close to. I consider it when you work at a community or home care or hospice you have all these adopted grandparents. Really just navigating how to be strong for them and their family members and trying to put that first in front of your own needs.

Kevin: Yeah, because they really do get close don't they?

Kelsie: Yeah, it can be tough but it's good. It's worth it.

Kevin: How did you come to this specific role that you're in now?

Kelsie: Previous to this I actually decided to take a little bit of time away from the very full-time senior industry roles and I ran a small painting business and so it was very flexible, I was able to be home with my little kids and after doing that for a while I was feeling the tug to get back into senior care. Once you're in it you just can't leave. I took a little hiatus and just started looking for a position and I found the board president had posted a job opening and met with them and a week later that was that.

Kevin: Wow. What would you say are the highlights of your role?

Kelsie: The highlights probably are connecting other professionals. I love networking, I love relationships and I love connecting other people and seeing them collaborate together to further their businesses. I think that's probably the biggest highlight is meeting people. That's what I do all week, I go out and meet people, I plan events, which I love to do as well and see people.

Kevin: Tailor made role.

Kelsie: Exactly. It's pretty perfect.

Kevin: One of the big things we see when we do reverse mortgages, is people want to stay in their homes as long as possible even if they have to start getting care while they're at home. They want to live at home as long as possible. How do you advise either the seniors you know or the vendors you work with to help them do that?

Kelsie: Oh gosh, I feel like we're pretty fortunate, especially in this community there are so many options out there, whether it's looking into home modification, home automation. There are so many neat companies coming around the corner where they all have that same purpose in mind, helping seniors stay in their home as long as possible. It's not always possible and that's okay too but if that is the goal there are so many things. You can have a maintenance company come out and make sure that it's tailored to your needs whether it's grab bars, wheelchair ramps, having a nice security system. There are all these technology things now where children that are still working can still help and make sure that Mom and Dad are safe at home by checking the app. "Did they take their medication? Did they check in? Are they okay? Do I have to stop over there?"

Of course there are many wonderful home care companies. You have non- medical, you've got skilled home care, there's home therapy, there's home hospice if it gets to that point. There are definitely many options.

Kevin: You're really the hub if you will, to introduce people to this vendor or that company.

Kelsie: Yeah, absolutely. Our main goal and mission at the Senior Resource Council really is to support and educate professionals so that they can serve our seniors better. Our end goal is that our community is taken care of and we do that by educating our professionals as well as helping them network and collaborate. If you look at our website, we have a list of all of our members so in a way it's a resource for people too. I get phone calls probably once a day from seniors that are looking for things because our name insinuates that we provide services. I say, "We don't provide services, but a lot of our members do. Feel free to check out our website."

Kevin: What are some of the most common mistakes you see seniors make as they approach or are in retirement?

Kelsie: I would say one of the things would be not doing enough research. I think a lot of times myself included we want to trust that first person that we talk to, whether it's a friend of a friend of a friend and they say, "You have to do it this way," and sometimes that gets people in trouble. I think being diligent about researching all the different avenues.

Kevin: Knowing their options.

Kelsie: Knowing their options I think is really big because you might have one person say, "No, you can't do this," and another person says, "You have to do this." I think it's good to have help from decision makers as well if they're fortunate enough to have close family. Children, grandchildren that might want to help. Taking all of that into consideration but doing what's best for them personally.

Kevin: How does your organization go about helping the seniors? You mentioned about all the different vendors you work with and the website. Is there anything else you want to mention to help seniors to work through some of these issues?

Kelsie: Yeah, I think our biggest thing that we try to do to give back to really show our community what resources are out there, is we do an expo every year. That's a nice way to showcase to our community what kind of resources are out there. It's a free event to the public. We highly encourage seniors and their family members, their decision makers, their kids, grandkids to come and check it out. There's a wide range of vendors there. We have some great speakers there. It's just a good educational event to really showcase what is out there because I think a lot of times people don't necessarily understand how many resources there really are. This is a great time for our members and anybody really to showcase what they do to our community.

Kevin: Kelsie, what do you like most about your business and what you do?

Kelsie: I think the best thing is the fact that I get to be in the senior industry, which is where my heart and passion is, and in a way give back to our seniors in our community. But also being on the professional side of it too, and educating, networking and just supporting the professionals. Because I'm one of the professionals that have been in it for quite a while, and I know that it's necessary and it's important that they're taken care of as well.

Kevin: Is there a product or service or something you offer that you wish more seniors knew about?

Kelsie: That's a tough question. Not the Senior Resource Council individually since we really serve the professionals, but I would say probably just our membership list on the website really because there are endless resources on there from all these amazing companies and just getting the word out there about that.

Kevin: How do you guys promote that?

Kelsie: It's really just on our website and I think that a lot of people find it when they're googling senior resources Colorado Springs. We're probably one of the first that comes up just because of our name. Sometimes people get us confused with the Senior Center which is fine. I'm able to refer people a lot to the Senior Center, the Area Agency on Aging which is huge in our community. They offer all the kinds of guidance that you would need as a senior.

Kevin: Who's an ideal client for you?

Kelsie: An ideal client for me would be any business that serves seniors in any capacity. It's not just your home cares and assisted living, it's mortgage companies, it's financial people, car dealerships that might serve seniors more than others, restaurants that offer senior discounts. Really any organization that wants to become what the big term right now is age friendly. Making our city age friendly through the innovations in aging, AARP and the Better Business Bureau are collaborating on doing that.

Kevin: Weren't we just named an age friendly city?

Kelsie: Yes. We are definitely working towards age friendly. Any company can go to the Better Business Bureau and get age friendly certified. They come to your place of business and do a walk through and make sure that you're considered age friendly and you get the designation. It's pretty neat.

Kevin: Okay, cool. These ideal clients, what's the first step you'd want them to take?

Kelsie: Probably meet with me. I really like to meet with businesses before they decide to join just to give them an idea of exactly what we do, what we offer and to make sure it would be a benefit to them.

Kevin: Okay. How do they find you normally, these ideal clients?

Kelsie: A lot of times it's word of mouth. We've grown significantly in the last couple of years and I think a lot of it really is current members that are inviting guests to come to our events that we have and that's probably the biggest way that they're finding us.

Kevin: Okay. How do you market? You mentioned you do some stuff on social media. How do you market your services to these potential ideal clients?

Kelsie: We have a pretty decent website that I manage. I keep it very updated and then our Facebook page is probably the next biggest thing. I post all of our events. I do tons of advertising for our members. If they've sponsored our expo I'll make sure to put a blurb about them on the website. Welcoming new members that we get. I try and keep that pretty active.

Kevin: As far as challenges, what's your biggest challenge you're facing right now?

Kelsie: I would say just making sure that we are as an organization keeping relevant to our members and making sure we're providing the best value possible. I don't know if that's a challenge. I guess it's something that I'm always keeping in the forefront in my mind.

Kevin: Yeah. No, it's good. Kelsie, what's the best advice you've ever received? It doesn't have to be about seniors, just life.

Kelsie: I would say I've gotten some good advice lately about releasing things from you that are not bringing you joy if that makes sense and opening up more space in your life for things that do bring you joy.

Kevin: That's good.

Kelsie: Yes.

Kevin: What would you like to share that I haven't already asked you?

Kelsie: Just getting the word out about us and our members. I don't see an end in sight as far as how many members we're going to have. I think almost every organization in Colorado Springs could benefit from an organization like the Senior Resource Council and we've got some really, really top-notch education that we're providing.

Kevin: Yes, I've been to some events. Where can our audience go to learn more about you and Senior Resource Council?

Kelsie: I would say probably our website would be the easiest, which is just SRCCOS.org and our Facebook page is pretty current and the best way is really just to come see me or give me a call. I like face to face better.

Kevin: Exactly. All right, thank you.

Kelsie: Thank you.

CLOSING THOUGHTS

Thank you for reading this book. I also want to say thank you again to the experts who so graciously agreed to be interviewed, and who shared so much valuable information. I hope you got as much out of reading the interviews as I did conducting them. My goal is for you to use this information, and reach out to these experts for their advice and insights.

Speaking of information, I'd like to wrap things up by sharing some important facts about reverse mortgages. Because unfortunately there's a lot of misinformation out there. And in many cases, it's keeping people from even considering applying for a reverse mortgage, and getting the cash flow that can make such a difference in their retirement lifestyle.

So let's clear up some common myths and misconceptions.

Myth: You lose title to your home
Fact: Homeowners always retain the title to their home, as long as they stay current on property taxes, homeowners insurance, homeowners' association dues, and any necessary home repairs.

Myth: This is a loan of last resort for people who have no other options
Fact: While many of the people who get reverse mortgages do need the cash flow, many people of means are also obtaining these loans because they want to put their equity to work for them. They're using the proceeds to buy a vacation home, travel, or other so-called luxury items.

Myth: Eligibility is limited
Fact: You're eligible if at least one of the homeowners is 62 or

older, it's their primary residence at least six months of the year, and they have at least 50% equity or more.

Myth: You can't leave your home to your children
Fact: The loan comes due when the last homeowner no longer lives in the home. (Death, nursing home, etc.) If there's equity in the home, the heirs sell the house and get the proceeds, or they can refinance and move in to the home. If the home is over leveraged, the borrower or heirs hands the keys over to HUD and walk away as the mortgage insurance makes up any shortfall.

Myth: It will affect taxes and Social Security
Fact: The proceeds from a reverse mortgage are usually tax-free. It is a loan, not income. You are still responsible for property taxes, insurance, and other home-related maintenance. And a reverse mortgage does not affect Social Security or Medicare.
Note: this is not tax advice, please consult your advisor.

Myth: Not every type of home is eligible
Fact: The following types of homes are eligible: single-family home, condo, townhouse, 2-4 unit properties, and manufactured homes built after June 1976.

Myth: You have to take the proceeds all at once
Fact: You have these options for taking the proceeds: lump sum, fixed monthly payments for a specific term, monthly payments for as long as you live in the home, a line of credit, or a combination of these options.

Myth: There are limits on how you can use the proceeds
Fact: HUD doesn't care how you spend the money. You can use it for to supplement your retirement cash flow to pay for necessities, or use it for lifestyle choices such as a second home. The only restriction is you cannot use it to buy an annuity.

Myth: It's risky

Fact: A reverse mortgage is a very safe loan. Numerous safeguards have been added since the program first began in 1987. Counseling is required, mortgage insurance is required, there are limits on rates and fees, and it's regulated by HUD.

I could go on. But the most important fact I can give you is this: reverse mortgages are safe, and for many senior citizens, this has made a huge difference in their retirement lifestyle. And it would be a shame if the wrong information kept people like you from joining them.

It's not a difficult process, but it can be intimidating. That's why I'm always happy to meet with someone who wants to know more about a reverse mortgage, answer their questions, and help them see how it would work in their specific situation. It's not a sales call. There's never any pressure or obligation. It's really just a chat.

If you'd like to have that type of conversation, maybe over a cup of coffee, call or email me any time. My contact information is below. If you have any questions, I'll answer them for you. You may end up deciding a reverse mortgage isn't the right thing for you. That's fine. I just want to make sure you make the right decision, based on the right information.

Here's to the retirement lifestyle you deserve!

Kevin A. Guttman
Reverse Mortgage Planner
NMLS #384936
877-251-9709
Kevin.Guttman@gmail.com
www.ReverseMortgageRevolution.com

www.ingramcontent.com/pod-product-compliance
Lightning Source LLC
Chambersburg PA
CBHW050158230526
45470CB00001B/146